TAX SAVING STRATEGIES

Tax Saving Strategies

FREEMAN LINDE

Dedication

To my wonderful wife, Kayla, who tirelessly supports me in all that I do. To my delightful daughters, Elodie and Emmelyn, and my super son, Soren, my pride and joy. This is for you.

Table of Contents

Dedication 3
Table of Contents 4

Book Bonus

Thank you for reading this book. You are entitled to the bonus material that accompanies this book. Go to:

TSSBook.com/Bonus

There, you can get your free access to become a RetireMember. That membership includes both exclusive and curated content.

Exclusive Content

This content is *only* available to RetireMembers and cannot be found anywhere else.

Curated Content

We've pulled together some of the most relevant content from across our platforms to make it easily accessible to you.

Book Bonuses for TSS
Your membership includes:

- **Tax Guide** – A quick reference guide to see the latest Tax Brackets and key figures. We update it annually, which is why it's not printed in the book.
- **Tax Decision Flow Charts** – Easy guides for figuring out if you can execute certain tax moves. These are updated annually.
- **Tax Calculators** – Easy methods for calculating things like how much of your Social Security is taxable or what your RMD is going to be.
- **Bonus Tax Workshop** – A full workshop, with workbook, on implementing these Tax Strategies.

This and much more is available, for free, with your Retire-Membership. Join today!

Disclaimer

I want to be clear on the front end to avoid disclaimers throughout this book.

This book is not tax, legal, or investment advice. This book is educational and not intended to be investment, legal, or tax advice or recommendations, whether direct or incidental. Again, this is not investment advice. Consult *your* financial, tax, and legal professionals for specific advice related to your specific situation.

Never take investment or tax advice from someone who doesn't know you and your specific situation.

Tax laws change frequently, and this book may become outdated. We will try to make updates as we can to keep it relevant.

All performance references are historical and do not guarantee future results. All indices are unmanaged and may not be invested in directly.

All investing involves risk, including the possible loss of principal. Investments are not FDIC insured, have no bank guarantee, and may lose value. (See Chapter Seven.)

With that out of the way, you can enjoy reading unhindered by constant caveats and disclaimers.

Part 1: Foundations

Chapter 1

The Goal

Why Do We Do Tax Planning?

Why are you reading this book? If you are going to commit three to five hours of your attention to me, what are you hoping to achieve? Let's ensure you are reading the right book and begin with the end in mind.

Your Largest Lifetime Expense

What is your largest expense that you will have in your lifetime? Most people will answer, "My house."

That's a fair answer. Between the purchase price of the home, the fees tacked on to buy it, the interest on the mortgage, and the likelihood that you will roll equity from your first home into one or more upgrades, many people pay a significant mortgage payment for thirty to forty years of their lives. A $300,000 mortgage at 5.5% ends up costing *$613,000*, and that doesn't count a down payment, property taxes, homeowner's insurance, or PMI. It's a significant expense.

But mortgages are eventually paid off. The majority of the expense goes away. So while significant, it's not the greatest.

Your largest lifetime expense is taxes. While many other expenses are seasonal, you will likely pay taxes for your entire working life *and* retirement. You may pay for college for four years, children for twenty years, and a mortgage for thirty, but you could pay taxes for *sixty*.

If taxes are your largest lifetime expense, doesn't it make sense to do something about it? Could it be worth your time to learn some strategies to minimize, reduce, mitigate, defer, or otherwise eliminate some of those taxes? That's where tax planning comes in.

Tax Planning vs Tax Preparation

Let's make a quick distinction between Tax Planning (which you can do anytime) and Tax Preparation (done in the spring for the previous year).

Tax Preparation is looking backward at what happened last year. It involves gathering tax forms, maintaining a historical record of income earned and expenses paid, and compiling this information to ensure the correct amount of taxes was paid last year.

Tax preparation often focuses on reducing last year's tax bill. Tax Preparers (DIYers or paid preparers) who focus solely on a single year often make strategic moves to reduce taxes for that year, even if it means paying more taxes over the long term. For example, they may contribute to a Traditional IRA to lower gross income for the year, when they should have contributed to a Roth IRA to lower their income for life.

Accurate Tax Preparation is critical. But it does not go far enough.

Tax Planning is looking forward. It uses current tax law and best estimates to predict future taxes. It incorporates the other parts of your financial plan to determine how to give yourself the best chance of paying the least amount of taxes, not just this year but over your *lifetime*.

If taxes are your largest expense and they can be reduced, you must plan to do so. If you can't plan it effectively yourself, you must hire someone to do it for you.

Generally, your tax preparer will not know enough to do proper tax planning. Not that their knowledge *taxes* are insufficient, but rather their knowledge of *you* is inadequate. A good CPA may have long-term tax-planning knowledge but only looks forward a few years. Most will prepare between 200 and 500 client tax returns over three months. They don't spend enough time with you and don't pull all the information necessary to do the tax planning. Has your CPA ever asked you for your 401(k) or Social Security statement? Exactly.

What the Goal is NOT

What *is* the goal of tax planning? First, let's cover what it's *not*.

The goal of Tax Planning is *not* to pay the least amount of taxes.

Wait, what? I thought that was the point. To minimize, reduce, mitigate, and eliminate taxes. Don't we want to pay the least amount of taxes possible?

Confusing the Goal with the Method is Madness

Recently, I was speaking with a young man in his twenties who was working on completing Dave Ramsey's Baby Steps program.

We'll call him John, because that was his name. John was about to pay off his car, and then he would be debt-free except for his mortgage. He then planned to use his free cash flow to make extra mortgage payments, aiming to pay off the mortgage as quickly as possible. He had a thirty-year mortgage from 2020 at a 3.0% interest rate. (At this time, money-market fund rates were around 4.1%.) He planned to pay off the last twenty-five years of his mortgage in fifteen years.

I said to him, "John, let me ask you this. What is the *goal*: to pay extra on the mortgage, or to pay off the house early?"

He replied, "To pay extra on the house."

"No, sorry, maybe I mis-spoke. What's the *goal*, not that *tactic*? What is the *goal*: paying extra on the mortgage, or paying off the house?"

He sounded less confident after a pause. "Paying extra on the mortgage?"

Apparently, I'm not great at the Socratic method.

"The *goal*," I explained, "is to have a paid-for house. The *method* or tactic you are using is to pay extra on the mortgage each month. Your goal *isn't* to pay extra on a mortgage. That's a means to an end. Your goal is the financial freedom of having a paid-off house in fifteen years instead of twenty-five."

He got it then.

Setting aside whether this is a good goal or not, I then challenged him on his method. With a 3% mortgage and money-market rates at 4.1%, he could make more money parking it with no risk than paying extra on his house. If he was also willing to invest all his free cash flow that he would have paid toward the mortgage into a good equity index fund, he could sell his investment in eight to twelve years during a bull market and pay off his remaining mortgage in one lump sum. Same goal achieved (a paid-

off house), but with a better *strategy*, he could achieve the goal in eight to twelve years
instead of fifteen.

If you have the wrong goal, you may achieve it. But you'll use methods that keep you from achieving the real goal.

Why Reducing Taxes is *Not* the Goal

Here's a scenario. I give you $100,000 in an after-tax brokerage account. How do you pay the least amount of taxes on this? It's easy! I'm going to show you in *one* move how to pay the least amount of taxes on $100,000. Forget all those fancy tax planning strategies. You only need this one tactic. Are you ready? (You might want to write this down or pull out a highlighter.)

Move it to a checking account and leave it there for the rest of your life. That $100,000 will earn zero interest or dividends, have zero realized capital gains, and generate zero ordinary income. Therefore, you will pay *$0* in taxes on that money. Not only did we minimize taxes on it, *we eliminated them!* You can't pay less than $0.

This is obviously absurd. Sure, we paid no taxes, *but we also earned no money!* But sometimes it takes the extreme end of a view to show the flaws in the shallow end.

If you want to pay zero taxes for your whole life, it's very easy. Just follow these four simple steps:

1. Earn no money to avoid income tax.
2. Own no investments to avoid interest and capital gains tax.
3. Live under a bridge to avoid property taxes.
4. Steal everything instead of buying to avoid sales tax.

Simple.

And as absurd as this may seem, I cannot stress enough how critical it is to understand this difference. **There are a host of strategies designed to "reduce taxes" that leave you *worse off*.** These strategies are terrible for you and are usually amazing for the wallets of those pedaling them. There are numerous strategies circulating on social media and promoted by financial services representatives, which I've dedicated chapter three to help you recognize and avoid them. **The goal of tax planning is *not* to pay the least amount of taxes.**

What IS the Goal?

The goal of tax planning is to maximize the amount of money *after* taxes.

Many strategies that primarily focus on reducing taxes do so by also reducing your overall after-tax net worth. When I do comprehensive financial planning for clients, they often end up paying *more* taxes. But they do so because they end up with more money. They may pay 10% more taxes over their lifetime and end up with 40% more money (with more of that being tax-free for their children and grandchildren than before).

I'm going to show you some amazing strategies for reducing taxes in this book, broken out into the following parts and chapters.

Part 1 – Foundations

Part 1 covers some foundational topics required for good tax planning, beginning with the end in mind in Chapter 1, which you're nearly done with.

Chapter 2 discusses the Tax Buckets, Deductions, and Credits. This chapter breaks down the various types of accounts and how they are taxed. It also breaks down the difference between deductions and credits. It's critical to know these things for good tax planning. If you already know them, you can skim or skip this optional chapter. Don't worry, I'll still give you credit for reading the whole book.

Chapter 3 covers the strategies you should avoid. In life, what *not* to do is often as important as what you do. Feel free to browse the subtitles of various strategies and only read the ones you're engaged in, that interest you, or are being promoted to you.

Part 2 – Tax Strategies

This is the main part of the book, where we dive into various strategies.

Chapter 4 covers Roth versus Traditional retirement. It discusses which contributions you should make and how to determine if Roth Conversions are the right choice. *This is a must-read for anyone who picks up this book.*

Chapter 5 handles Brokerage Accounts. If you have non-retirement investments, this chapter is for you. If you don't, skip it entirely.

Chapter 6 discusses tax planning for Social Security and medical insurance. If you haven't claimed Social Security yet and are over age 50, you will want to read the section. And if you're hoping to retire before age 65, you'll want to read part two of this chapter.

Chapter 7 covers charitable gifting. How do you give more to charities and less to the government? Are there ways to shift money away from the IRS and to your church with no impact on take-home pay? Yes! I can't wait to share! If you're charitably inclined or tithe to your church, you definitely want to read this chapter. And if you don't give much, read it anyway. We'll show some cool ways to start.

Chapter 8 discusses legacy taxes—who pays taxes on your money when you're gone. It will include strategies on how to limit these multi-generational taxes, and how beginning with the end in mind will shape your current tax planning.

Part 3 – Part of a Plan

Good tax planning can only be done as part of a comprehensive plan. Each part of the plan affects all the others.

Chapter 9 is a primer on maximizing your money, not just minimizing your taxes. If the goal is to maximize your money after taxes, we'll need strategies on how to do this. WARNING: More money will produce more taxes. However, combining these strategies will lead to a lower tax *rate*, even if you pay more in tax dollars on your multiplied investments.

Finally, **Chapter 10 covers putting it all into action.** For those who love the strategies but prefer not to implement them themselves, it will show you how to find a good tax strategist to work with.

Book Bonus

As a thank-you for getting this book, I want to offer some bonuses to help you on your Tax Savings journey.

I create a lot of free content across YouTube, Podcasts, and a website under the brand RetireMentorship. The purpose of the content is to be your mentor to and through retirement, helping you retire successfully *and stay* successfully retired. I also have Retire*Membership*, additional *free* content for subscribers.

I've created several specific bonuses for this book that are available to all my RetireMembers at no cost. All you need to do is go to RetireMembership.com and click the link to join. You'll then get instant access to:

- RetireMentorship Tax Guide to reference and quickly find your tax brackets, thresholds, and phaseouts.

Who Am I

Why should you listen to me? Let me give you the short answer.

I am a Certified Financial Planner, which is the gold standard for comprehensive advice. I founded La Crosse Financial Planning and specialize in helping folks retire successfully *and stay* successfully retired. I am an expert in how all of one's financial life fits together and how each aspect impacts all the others.

I am a fee-only fiduciary. I'm not here to sell you any products or make any commissions. My work with my clients is always and only in their best interests, and I bring that same focus to you as you read this book.

I am an Enrolled Agent, which is the federal license to give tax advice and represent taxpayers before the IRS. This is not to be confused with IRS Agent—I'm on your side of the table.

(How does an Enrolled Agent (EA) compare to a Certified Public Accountant (CPA)? CPAs get most of their extensive training on corporate accounting, where the three-part EA exam focuses exclusively on tax returns and tax practice. While a CPA knows worlds more than I do about audits and ledgers, we have a lot of the same training on personal taxes.)

In other words, I'm a financial, investment, and retirement expert, *and* a tax expert. I understand and can advise on the impact of everything else on taxes, and the impact of taxes on everything else.

Many people have had the experience of asking their financial advisor a tax question only to hear, "I'm sorry, I can't give tax advice. Go ask your CPA." Then they ask their CPA and hear, "I'm sorry, I don't know what else you have going on. Go ask your Financial Advisor." This siloed advice between investments and taxes leads to many issues and additional taxes. I do both.

I see a lot of investment advice peddled out there that ignores the taxes, and a lot of "tax strategies" that ignore proper investing and planning. I'm going to teach you how to do both.

Who This Book is For

I've read a lot of customer-facing tax books, and they are all quite boring. Here's why: They try to be a comprehensive tax book for everyone. This leads to several problems:

- Broad Audience. They try to give tax strategies to everyone from college grads to retiring employees to mid-career business owners. In speaking to everyone, they reach no one.
- Repetitive Examples: They are constantly telling you all the possible scenarios, even though only one applies to you. For example, they may list the Single, Married Filing Jointly, and Head of Household tax rates for every example, when all you care about is the MFJ rates.
- Long and Boring. Because these books are trying to cover so much, they are hard to get through.

We're going to fix these issues. **This book is for couples aged 55-75.** You can still gain a lot of insight if this does not describe you perfectly, but the farther you are away from this, the less it will apply. This narrow focus allows me to be more impactful in a few ways.

- **Relevant Topics**. We won't waste time with business deductions and first-time home-buying credits. If you're in

this age range, nearly everything in the book will apply to you.
- **Specific Examples.** We will use specific examples of couples like you and only refer to Married Filing Jointly rates to keep the book flow readable. Note, if you're single, this does not exclude you. I think it's tacky to have to elucidate the tax rates every time. You can generally cut the tax numbers in half for single rates.
- **Quick and Digestible.** We'll keep the chapters short and give you summaries and action items at the end of each chapter.

Who this Book is NOT For

This book is not for know-it-alls. Before I explain that, let me ask you a question.

On a scale of 1-10, how much do you know about taxes and tax strategy?

- 1 would be "I know next to nothing. Taxes come out of my paycheck, and I hand off tax documents to my accountant each year."
- 10 would be "I know almost everything. I could be a tax and financial planning professional, but I like my job better."

This book is for people who rate themselves 1-6, with the goal of getting them to rate themselves 4-7.

If you are a 7-9, and the kind of person who is going to go on Amazon and give a 1-star review because "I didn't learn anything new," then this book is not for you. If you are already well-read and well-educated on this topic, you need to read advanced textbooks or get a tax designation to learn more. I'll gladly refund your money.

Financial Fatigue

Before we go any further, I want to prepare you for something that almost everyone experiences when they begin to take tax planning seriously: financial fatigue.

Right now, you're likely energized. You see that taxes are your largest lifetime expense. You see that smart strategies could help you keep more of what you earn. The idea of maximizing your after-tax wealth is motivating. But motivation is easy at the beginning, when the concepts are simple, and the upside feels obvious.

Then come the details.

Tax brackets stack on top of each other. Social Security becomes partially taxable. IRMAA thresholds create hidden marginal rates. Roth conversions interact with capital gains. Deductions phase out. Strategies that look brilliant in isolation become complicated when integrated into a full plan. The math is not impossible—but it is layered.

This is where many readers enter what psychologists call the Dunning–Kruger Effect. At first, confidence is high because the basic ideas feel straightforward. Then comes the "valley of despair," where the complexity becomes visible and confidence drops. It's not because you're incapable. It's because you're now seeing the whole board.

Financial fatigue sets in when enthusiasm meets complexity.

You may feel the urge to put the book down and "come back to it later." If that happens, I want you to recognize it for what it is: a natural response to depth, not a signal to quit. When you feel that resistance, skip ahead to the Financial Fatigue section in Chapter

10. I'll remind you there why the work is worth it—and how to simplify it.

The goal is not to master every tax code provision. The goal is to understand enough to make wise decisions, avoid costly mistakes, and either implement these strategies yourself or confidently work with someone who can.

Complexity does not mean impossibility. It means opportunity—for those willing to push through it.

"Case Studies"

Throughout the book, we will also provide ongoing case studies of three different couples. I will introduce them all here, and then show you, throughout the book, how each strategy would apply to their case. If you identify with one or two of the couples, you can just read their case studies and skip the others. Or you can read them all and have a more rounded view of taxes.

Couple 1: Steve & Rachel

Age & Status: Steve (52) and Rachel (54) are both in their prime income-earning years. Steve is an attorney, and Rachel is a medical director.

Income & Expenses: Steve & Rachel earn about $450,000 in gross annual income and are maxing out their retirement accounts.

Assets & Liabilities: Steve & Rachel have the following in accounts:

	Steve	Rachel
401(k)s	$850,00	$1,200,000

IRAs	$300,000	$150,000
Roths	$200,000	$130,000
Brokerage (Jt)	$150,000	
Savings	$50,000	

Children & Legacy: Steve & Rachel have two children in college, and they are funding their education. They give charitably, though not as much as they'd like, because they feel their expenses are high. They plan to leave their money equally to their children.

Couple 2: Chuck & Diane

Age & Status: Chuck (63) and Diane (62) are about to retire. Chuck is a high-level manager for a mid-sized company, and Diane is a nurse now (though she took many years off to raise kids).

Income & Expenses: Chuck & Diane earn about $238,000 in gross annual income and are maxing out their retirement accounts.

Assets & Liabilities: Chuck & Diane have the following in accounts:

	Chuck	Diane
401(k)s	$370,000	$450,000
IRAs	$1,900,000	$780,000
Roths	$0	$0
Brokerage (Jt)	$0	

Savings	$0

Children & Legacy: Chuck & Diane have three children grown children and four grandchildren. They give and plan to leave their money to their children and some to their grandchildren.

Couple 3: Bob & Sue

Age & Status: Bob (71) and Sue (70) are both retired. Bob was a Civil Engineer, and Sue was a teacher.

Income & Expenses: Bob & Sue have $50,000 in Social Security Income and another $50,000 in federal and state pensions. Their annual expenses total $100,000, which allows them to live comfortably without touching their retirement assets.

Assets & Liabilities: Bob has $600,000 in his Thrift Savings Plan (TSP, a 401(k) for federal employees), and Sue has $200,000 in her 403(b) (a 401(k) for non-profits).

	Bob	Sue
TSP & 403(b)	$600,000	$200,000
IRAs	$0	$0
Roths	$0	$0
Brokerage (Jt)	$80,000	
Savings	$40,000	

Children & Legacy: They have four adult children, all of whom are doing well. They tithe on their income and plan to leave their assets equally to their children.

You may find that you identify with one couple for their age, and another for their income or net worth. You should be able to apply the principles and strategies of this book and the examples of these case studies to your own life.

The Challenge

I'm going to challenge you. Don't just read this book. Here's what I mean.

Learning may be described as consuming information that leads to a change in behavior. If you "learn" something but it doesn't affect your life at all, did you learn anything?

There is no difference between those who can't read and those who don't. It can also be said that there is no difference between those who read and don't change, and those who never read.

Thus, **you only get credit for reading this book if you do something different as a result—no action: no credit.** If you do nothing after reading this, you didn't learn anything. And if you can spend hours reading a book without learning anything, you may not be that intelligent by our definition above. Don't be dumb. Learn something; do something.

To be clear, the "doing something" may be to go get more information. It may be getting the book bonus and watching the workshop. It may be subscribing to my YouTube channel. There may be additional actions you take to learn more before big actions are taken. But this is all to promote the big actions.

I've included two elements in this book to support your learning. The last page of each chapter will include a Chapter Summary of the key points of that chapter. These summaries will reinforce what you've just read and drive home the takeaways. It will also serve as an easy way for you to review the book in the future.

I will also include Action Items. These are specific ways you can apply what you are learning and thus prove that you did, in fact, learn.

You can read all the summaries and remember the book's central messages in about 5-10 minutes. Let's dive in!

Tax Rates, Buckets, Deductions, and Credits

Chapter Summary

- Taxes are likely your largest lifetime expense—larger than your mortgage, larger than college, and potentially lasting longer than your career. Because of that, tax planning deserves the same intentionality as investing, estate planning, or retirement income design.
- Tax preparation looks backward. Tax planning looks forward. Preparation focuses on what happened last year; planning models what could happen over the next 10, 20, or 30 years and seeks to minimize lifetime taxes—not just this year's bill.
- The goal of tax planning is not to pay the least amount of taxes. The goal is to maximize the amount of money you have after taxes over your lifetime. Strategies that reduce taxes but also reduce growth, flexibility, or long-term wealth miss the point entirely.
- Confusing a method with the goal leads to poor decisions. Reducing taxes is not the same as building wealth. Always

measure strategies by after-tax net worth, not by this year's refund.
- Part 1 lays the foundation (tax buckets, deductions, and mistakes to avoid).
- Part 2 walks through specific, practical tax strategies.
- Part 3 integrates tax strategy into a comprehensive plan.
- You have also met three case-study couples—Steve & Rachel, Chuck & Diane, and Bob & Sue—who represent different ages, income levels, and tax challenges. As you move through the book, watch how the same strategy produces different outcomes depending on age, account structure, and timing.
- Finally, expect financial fatigue. Initial confidence often gives way to complexity. That is normal. If you feel overwhelmed, do not quit—skip ahead to the Financial Fatigue section in Chapter 10 for perspective, then return and keep going

Chapter 2
Foundational Knowledge for All Tax Planning

Before we dive into the fun tax-savings strategies, we need to ensure we are on the same page regarding some foundational aspects of tax planning. If you feel like you understand all of this already, minimally browse the headlines and read any sections you are fuzzy on. But for most of us, a full recap is beneficial.

We're going to cover the various tax types and buckets, and review the difference between deductions and credits.

Tax Types

There are a few different ways we are taxed, and it is important to know the differences if we are going to plan for them. Let's review.

Ordinary Income Taxes

Ordinary income taxes (OIT) are the regular income taxes that we all think about. These are the main taxes that get reconciled on our federal and state income tax returns, and the taxes that get taxed at the standard rates.

Ordinary Income Tax Rates are the tax rates we all think about. They are as follows for Married Filing Jointly in 2026 (Other rates are in the Tax Guide, which can be found in the bonus materials).

- 10%
- 12%
- 22%
- 24%
- 32%
- 35%
- 37%

Notice the large jumps between 12% and 22%, and between 24% and 32%. Those are our largest planning opportunities.

Ordinary income (and the taxes associated with it) comes from multiple sources.

Earned Income is the income we, well, earn. You receive this through your paychecks as an employee (reported on your W-2), or through income you keep from independent contracting (reported on your 1099s). Earned income is also subject to Social Security and Medicare taxes (covered shortly). Taxes are generally withheld from earned income or paid in quarterly estimates.

Interest Income comes from bank accounts, CDs, money market accounts, and other sources that generate income. Taxes generally cannot be withheld from interest income, and thus can be a source of owing additional taxes when you file.

Retirement Income includes distributions from pre-tax retirement accounts (IRAs, 401(k)s, etc.), annuities, and pensions. Taxes can often be withheld from these distributions or paid from another source.

Social Security taxability (how much of your Social Security Income is taxable) depends on your other income. It may be either completely tax-free, up to 85% taxable, or somewhere in between. We'll cover how to calculate that and how much of it is taxable in another chapter, but whatever is taxable is taxed as Ordinary Income. Taxes can be withheld.

Other Income can also be taxed at these rates, even if it does not fall into one of the above categories. This includes rental income, business owner profits, and other types.

Social Security & Medicare Taxes

Earned income is also subject to Social Security and Medicare taxes. The total tax for these is:

- Social Security: 12.4%
- Medicare: 2.9%

As an employee, you pay half of these taxes as FICA taxes, and your employer pays the other half (known as payroll taxes). If you are self-employed, you pay both (known as Self-Employment Taxes).

Note that there are many deductions for Ordinary Income Taxes, but almost none for Social Security and Medicare Taxes. The income that is subject to Social Security is capped ($184,500 *per person* in 2026), while there is no cap on Medicare Taxes.

If you look at your W2, you will see:

- Box 1: Income subject to Ordinary Income. (Some deductions may have already been taken to reduce this number.)
- Box 3: Income subject to Social Security. This will be the lesser of your gross income or the cap.
- Box 5: Income subject to Medicare. This is your true gross income.

For some people, these numbers may all be the same, while for others, they may all be different.

Capital Gains

Capital gains taxes are paid on the growth of investments held outside retirement or tax-deferred accounts. If you buy an investment for $1,000, this is your cost basis (what you paid for it). If you sell it later for $1,500, you have a $500 capital gain. This gain is subject to taxes, but at a different rate than earned income. The government wants to incentivize investing, so it grants a different set of tax rates for these investments.

Capital Gains Rates differ from Ordinary Income Rates. They are:

- 0% if your *taxable* income is less than about $100,000.
- 15% if your *taxable* income is between ~$100,000-$600,000.
- 20% if your *taxable* income is more than $600,000.

Note that capital gains rates are applied to the gains, but that the *rate* you pay is based on your *taxable* income. Income subject to capital gains sits on top of ordinary income. We'll cover this more in Chapter 5.

Long-Term Capital Gains are gains on investments you've held for *more than* one year. If you buy an investment on April 15, 2026, and sell it on April 16th, 2027, or later, then you've held it for more than one year, and it is considered a Long-Term capital gain. These gains are subject to the capital gains rates.

Short-Term Capital Gains are gains on investments held for *one year or less*. If you sold the investment above a day earlier, it would be considered a short-term capital gain. Short-term capital gains are subject to ordinary income taxes, not capital gains rates.

Dividends

Company stocks, equity mutual funds, and exchange-traded funds pay dividends. These dividends are either ordinary or qualified (if held for the right period and from a qualifying source). Your 1099-DIV will tell you how much of each you have.

Qualified Dividends are taxed at capital gains rates. These dividends are obviously preferable. The same income stacking rules apply to qualified dividends as they do to long-term capital gains when determining the rate you are paying based on taxable income.

Ordinary Dividends are taxed at ordinary income tax rates. Note that when you see "Ordinary Dividends" on your 1040, this is inclusive of "Qualified Dividends." Think of this line as "Total Dividends," and you will need to subtract out Qualified Dividends to the left to find out how much is taxed at ordinary income rates.

Extra Taxes

There are a few other taxes you may have to pay.

Net Investment Income Taxes (NIIT) are an extra 3.8% that you would pay on your investment income. This is income from Interest, Dividends, Capital Gains, and Rental and business profit income. This extra tax is assessed on all investment income above the threshold when your Modified Adjusted Gross Income (MAGI) crossed $250,000.

Nerd Note: NIIT is based on MAGI, not taxable income, and the threshold does not increase. It's also one of the rare times when the single amount is not half of the Married Filing Jointly amount. The threshold for Singles is $200,000. If you have a lot of investment income, you may be better off being single.

Additional Medicare Tax is an additional 0.09% deducted from earned income above $250,000 in a year. It doesn't appear on your tax return, but it does appear on your W-2.

Income Related Medicare Adjustment Amount (IRMAA) is the additional Medicare Part B and D premiums you pay per month when your MAGI goes over certain thresholds. This is calculated in the tax return, but does not show up in a tax return. It simply increases your Medicare premium two years later.

Why the delay? If your 2025 income would put you over the threshold to pay more Medicare Premiums, the IRS won't know about it until you file taxes in the spring of 2026. Then they will make it active for 2027 Premiums. Thus, 2025 income affects 2027 premiums (2-year delay).

Marginal, Effective, and Marginal Effective Rates

If you want to pay less in taxes, you *must* understand the difference between marginal and effective tax rates.

Your **Marginal Tax Rate** (or marginal tax bracket) is the tax rate you pay on your last taxable dollar. Everyone pays 0% on at least the first $15,000 of income (per person, due to the standard deduction). Then everyone will pay 10%, then 12%, then 22% as their income increases. The highest tax bracket your taxable income falls into is your *marginal* tax rate.

Your **Effective Tax Rate** is the average rate you pay. You get this by dividing your total tax (not your refund, but your actual total taxes owed) by your gross income.

Examples (numbers rounded):

- Steve & Rachel had the following in 2026:
    - Gross Income: $450,000
    - Taxable Income: $410,000
    - Total Tax: $84,000
    - **Marginal Tax Rate: 32%**
        - That bracket is for Taxable Income over: $403,550 in 2026
    - **Effective Tax Rate: 18.67%**
        - $84,000 / $450,000 = 0.1867 ◈ 18.67%
- Chuck and Diane had the following in 2026:
    - Gross Income: $238,000
    - Taxable Income: $200,000
    - Total Tax: $33,000
    - **Marginal Tax Rate: 22%**
        - That bracket is for Taxable Income over: $100,800 in 2026
    - **Effective Tax Rate: 13.9%**
        - $33,000 / $238,000 = 0.139 ◈ 13.9%

Your **Marginal Effective Rate** is the *full tax rate* you would pay on the next dollar of income, including all additional taxes it may trigger.

Example: Let's say Bob & Sue were ending 2026 with an AGI of $217,200 and taxable income of $185,000. That would put them in the 22% marginal tax bracket. They could do a Roth Conversion of another $1,000 at 22%, which is the *marginal rate*. But doing so would also push their MAGI over $218,000 and trigger the first IRMAA threshold, costing them an extra $1,944. So, on a $1,000 conversion, they would be paying:

- 22% Fed Taxes: $220
- IRMAA for 2: $1,944
- Total Tax: $2,164
- **Effective Marginal Rate: 216%**

That's right. Bob & Sue would be paying an 216% on that $1,000 conversion! Now, it's only that high on that $1,000. If they did a larger conversion, the Effective Marginal Rate would average out to a lower number. But it would still be more than the 22% marginal rate they think they are paying because of the IRMAA charge.

More on this later, but it's an important feature.

Tax Buckets

Where you store your money determines how it is taxed. There are several types of accounts, or "buckets" as many planners call them, where we can invest our money.

Account Taxation

There are three places your money can be taxed in an account. Let's break those down and then give examples.

Contributions are the money you are putting into an account. Contributions to an account can be made with:

- Pre-tax money
- Deductible post-tax money, or

- Non-deductible post-tax money.

Growth refers to when and if the growth of your money is taxed while it is in the account. It can be:

- Tax deferred, meaning that you don't pay any taxes on interest, dividends, and gains as long as it is in the account.
- Taxable, meaning that you do pay taxes on interest and dividends annually, and on gains when they are incurred.

Distributions are when you withdraw money from an account. These distributions can be:

- Full Taxable, meaning the full distribution is added to gross income for the year.
- Tax-free, meaning it typically doesn't even hit your taxable return.
- Tax Neutral, meaning you've already paid taxes on the interest, dividends, and gains, and therefore distributing the cash from the account has no additional impact.

Account Type

Let's look at the four account types and their taxation.
Traditional retirement accounts have these characteristics:

- **Contributions are pre-tax** to your employer-sponsored 401(k), 403(b), 457, SIMPLE IRA, or Deferred Compensation plans. The contributions never even oappear on your tax return (and are counted in your W2). They can also make **tax-deductible** contributions into an Individual Retirement Account (IRA). The difference between pre-tax

and tax-deductible is how it hits your tax return. The result is the same.
- **Growth is tax-deferred.** As long as the money remains in the account, you do not pay any annual taxes on any of the money in the account.
- **Distributions are 100% taxable** and are added to gross income on your tax return.

Roth retirement accounts have these characteristics:

- **Contributions are post-tax** to your employer-sponsored 401(k), 403(b), 457(b) plans, or Roth SIMPLE IRAs, as well as to Roth IRAs. There is no deduction, and you make the contributions with money that has already been taxed.
- **Growth is tax-deferred.** As long as the money remains in the account, you do not pay any annual taxes on any of the money in the account.
- **Distributions are 100% Tax Free** *if you follow the rules.*

Roth Distribution Rules

Roth accounts are incredibly powerful. But they are not magical. They come with rules. Understanding these rules is especially important for couples doing conversions in their fifties.

Age 59½ Rule. For both Traditional and Roth retirement accounts, age **59½** is the key threshold.

- Distributions before 59½ are generally subject to a **10% early withdrawal penalty**.
- After 59½, distributions are penalty-free (though Traditional distributions are still taxable).

With Roth accounts, the penalty rules apply differently depending on whether you are withdrawing **contributions, conversions, or growth.**

Withdrawal Ordering Rules (Roth IRAs). Roth IRAs follow strict ordering rules when money comes out:

- **Regular Contributions** come out first.
- **Converted dollars** come out next (first-in, first-out by conversion year).
- **Growth (earnings)** comes out last.

This is extremely important.

- Regular Roth IRA contributions can always be withdrawn tax-free and penalty-free, because you already paid taxes on them.
- Converted dollars may be subject to penalties if withdrawn too soon.
- Earnings may be subject to both tax and penalty if withdrawn improperly.

The 5-Year Clock. There are actually two separate 5-year rules.

1. The Roth IRA 5-Year Rule for Earnings
To withdraw earnings tax-free, you must:

- Be age 59½ (or meet another qualifying event such as death or disability), **and**
- Have had a Roth IRA open for at least 5 years.

The 5-year clock starts January 1 of the year you make your first Roth IRA contribution.

2. The 5-Year Rule for Each Conversion

Each Roth conversion has its own 5-year clock for penalty purposes.

- If you convert money at age 55 and withdraw those converted dollars at age 57, the IRS may assess a 10% penalty on that amount—even though you already paid income tax on the conversion.
- Once you reach age 59½, the conversion penalty risk largely disappears.

Non-Qual**ified (Brokerage)** Accounts

Non-qualified accounts—also called brokerage accounts, joint investment accounts, or after-tax accounts—are investment accounts that are not retirement accounts. There are no contribution limits, no age restrictions, and no required minimum distributions. They are extremely flexible, but they do not receive special tax sheltering like retirement accounts.

Non-Qualified accounts have the following characteristics:

Contributions are non-deductible post-tax money. You receive no tax break when you contribute. The money has already been included in gross income and taxed.

Growth is taxable.

- Interest is taxed annually at ordinary income tax rates.
- Ordinary (non-qualified) dividends are taxed annually at ordinary income tax rates.
- Qualified dividends are taxed at capital gains rates.
- Capital gains are taxed when realized (when you sell an investment for more than your cost basis).
- If you do not sell, you do not incur capital gains taxes.

Distributions are partially tax-neutral.

- Your original contributions (cost basis) are not taxed again.
- If you sell investments to generate cash, any realized gains are taxable.
- If you sell at a loss, you may generate a deductible capital loss.

Because of their flexibility, non-qualified accounts are powerful planning tools in retirement. They allow you to control the timing of gains, harvest losses, manage taxable income, and potentially receive a step-up in basis at death for heirs. While they lack the upfront deduction of Traditional accounts and the tax-free growth of Roth accounts, they are an essential third bucket in a comprehensive tax strategy.

Health Savings Accounts (HSA)

Health Savings Accounts (HSAs) are unique. They are the only accounts in the tax code that can legitimately receive triple tax benefits if used properly. To contribute to an HSA, you must be enrolled in a High Deductible Health Plan (HDHP). HSAs have the following characteristics:

Contributions are pre-tax or tax-deductible.

- Payroll contributions avoid federal income tax, state income tax (in most states), and Social Security and Medicare taxes.
- Direct contributions are an above-the-line deduction that reduces Adjusted Gross Income (AGI).

Growth is tax-deferred.

- Interest, dividends, and capital gains inside the account are not taxed annually.

Distributions are tax-free if used for qualified medical expenses.

- Qualified expenses include deductibles, copays, prescriptions, Medicare Part B and Part D premiums, and many other healthcare costs.
- You are not required to reimburse yourself in the same year the expense is incurred.
- You may pay expenses out of pocket, allow the HSA to grow for years, and reimburse yourself later tax-free.

If HSA funds are withdrawn for non-medical expenses:

- Before age 65, the withdrawal is subject to ordinary income tax and a penalty.
- After age 65: the penalty disappears, and withdrawals are taxed as ordinary income (similar to a Traditional IRA).

Because healthcare is one of the largest expenses in retirement, HSAs function as more than insurance tools. Used strategically, they reduce taxes today, grow tax-free, and can fund future medical expenses entirely tax-free, making them one of the most powerful planning accounts available.

Tax Deductions & Credits

Let's quickly review the difference between tax deductions and tax credits. But first, let's explore the tax structure.

The Structure of a Tax Return

Most people don't look at their tax return, just at the result: how much of a refund they are getting. This is a mistake. **The most important line on a tax return is not your Refund Amount, but your Total Taxes.** Let's briefly look at how a tax return is laid out.

The structure of a tax return is:

- Gross Income from various sources
- +/- Adjustments (additions or certain deductions)
- = **Adjusted Gross Income***
- - Standard or Itemized Deductions
- = **Taxable Income***
- * Various tax rates
- = **Tax** (before credits)
- - Credits
- + Additional Taxes
- = **Total Tax***
- - Withholdings and Estimated Payments
- = Refund/Amount Due

A few important lines to look at:

- Adjusted Gross Income (AGI) is important for tax planning because eligibility for credits and deductions is often tied to AGI or "Modified" AGI (MAGI).
- Taxable Income determines your Marginal Tax Rate. This is the number to which the federal tax rates are applied.
- Total Tax is the amount you actually pay.

Less Important:

- Tax Refund/Amount Due. Generally, you want this number to be between $0 and $2,000 refund.

Now we'll look at how we get from Gross Income to Total Tax by looking at deductions and credits.

Tax Deductions
Tax Deductions are reductions in your taxable income.
Example:

Chuck & Diane had a gross income of $238,000, taxable income of $205,800 in 2026, putting them in the 22% tax bracket with a total tax of $34,700. A $10,000 deduction would have reduced their taxable income by an additional $10,000, therefore reducing their federal taxes by $2,200.

Deductions are classified into two categories.

- Above-the-line deductions are the adjustments to gross income that derive Adjusted Gross Income (AGI). These are worth more than the others, because they lower AGI (which also lowers taxable income). Examples Include:
  - Deductible Traditional IRA contributions
  - Health Savings Account (HSA) contributions
  - Health insurance premiums for the self-employed
  - One-half of self-employment taxes
  - Qualified retirement plan contributions for the self-employed (SEP-IRA, SIMPLE, Solo 401(k))
  - Student loan interest (subject to income limits)
  - Alimony paid (for divorces finalized before 2019)
- Below-the-line deductions are reductions in taxable income only, not AGI. Examples include:
  - Standard Deduction
  - Itemized Deductions (more in Chapter 8)
  - Qualified Business Income Deduction

Deductions are great because they lower your taxable income and, therefore, your tax for a given year. But be careful! Many deductions are tax deferrals, not tax reductions. You are reducing taxes this year only to pay them later. And you end up paying more later! Remember, **the goal is not to pay the least amount of taxes last year, but to have the most money after paying over your lifetime.**

Tax Credits

Tax credits are dollar-for-dollar reductions in your taxes due. Example:

Chuck & Diane had a gross income of $238,000, taxable income of $205,800 in 2026, putting them in the 22% tax bracket with a total tax of $34,700. A $10,000 *credit* would have reduced their *taxes* by $10,000. A $10,000 tax reduction is better than a $2,200 reduction. Credits > Deductions.

Flip back to the tax structure and make sure you see where deductions and credits apply.

You now have some foundational knowledge of how taxes work and some of the essential building blocks of tax planning. Feel free to return to this chapter to refresh on anything. Now let's get into the fun!

Chapter Summary

- Ordinary Income is taxed at progressive rates (10%–37% in 2026). The largest planning jumps occur between 12% and 22%, and 24% and 32%.
- Capital Gains and Qualified Dividends are taxed at preferential rates (0%, 15%, or 20%), but those rates are determined by your total taxable income.
- Earned income is subject to Ordinary Income AND Social Security and Medicare taxes.
- Extra taxes such as NIIT, Additional Medicare Tax, and IRMAA can significantly increase your true marginal rate.
- Your Marginal Tax Rate is the rate on your next dollar of income. Your Effective Tax Rate is your average rate. Your Marginal Effective Rate includes hidden triggers, such as IRMAA.
- Where you store money determines how it is taxed.
- Traditional accounts: Pre-tax in, tax-deferred growth, fully taxable out.
- Roth accounts: After-tax in, tax-deferred growth, tax-free out (if rules are followed).
- Non-qualified accounts: After-tax in, taxable growth, tax-neutral distributions with taxable gains.

- HSA accounts: Pre-tax in, tax-deferred growth, tax-free out for medical expenses.
- Deductions reduce taxable income. Credits reduce taxes dollar-for-dollar. Credits are generally more powerful than deductions.
- The most important number on your tax return is not your refund. It is your Total Tax.

You now have the foundational framework for the rest of this book. Every strategy we discuss from here forward is simply a way of moving money between buckets, managing income thresholds, or applying deductions and credits more intelligently.

Action Items

1. Pull out your most recent federal tax return.
   - Highlight: Gross Income, Adjusted Gross Income (AGI), Taxable Income, and Total Tax.
2. Calculate your Effective Tax Rate.
   - Divide Total Tax by Gross Income.
   - Write the percentage in the margin.
3. Identify your Marginal Tax Bracket.
   - Use your Taxable Income and the Tax Guide from the Book Bonus to determine your current bracket.
4. List your current account balances by bucket.
   - Total in Traditional accounts
   - Total in Roth accounts
   - Total in Non-qualified accounts
   - Total in HSA accounts
5. Estimate your Marginal Effective Rate.
   - Are you close to a capital gains threshold?
   - Are you near an IRMAA threshold?

- Would one more dollar of income trigger an additional tax or premium increase?
6. Ask yourself this question:
    - If the goal is to maximize money after taxes over your lifetime, are your current savings and withdrawal strategies aligned with that goal?

Do not skip these steps. The strategies in the coming chapters will only make sense if you understand your current tax picture first.

Terrible Tax Strategies

Chapter 3
Tax Savings Mistakes to Avoid

In chapter 1, we established the goal: not to pay the least amount of taxes but have the most money after taxes. That distinction changes everything.

If the goal is to simply reduce taxes this year, there are dozens of tactics that would work. You could defer income, you could accelerate deductions, you could buy products wrapped in tax-deferral language, you could chase right off the way some people chase clearance racks.

Remember the absurd example from Chapter 1. If you truly want to eliminate taxes, eliminate income and move your money to a checking account, where it earns nothing. Congratulations! You've reduced your taxes to zero and destroyed your wealth in the process.

Reducing taxes is easy. Maximizing after-tax wealth is hard.

And here's the reality: it's just as important to avoid terrible tax strategies as it is to adopt good ones. **Avoiding blunders is as powerful as adopting brilliance.**

In investing, we know this intuitively. Avoiding a catastrophic loss often matters more than capturing an extraordinary gain. The same principle applies to tax planning. A single misguided strategy, implemented for years, can quietly erode hundreds of thousands of dollars from your lifetime wealth.

The problem is that many tax savings strategies sound smart. They are marketed well. They often produce a short-term benefit that feels like a win. Sometimes they can even generate a refund. But beneath the surface, they may:

- Shift taxes into higher rate years.
- Create unnecessary complexity.
- Trigger hidden fees and surrender charges.
- Lock up capital.
- Reduce long-term growth.
- Increased taxes for the surviving spouses or heirs

In other words, **they lower the tax bill while lowering your net worth.** That is the exact opposite of the goal.

For couples over 50, the stakes are even higher. You are approaching – or already in – the phase of your life where Required Minimum Distributions (RMDs), Social Security taxation, Medicare premium surcharges (IRMAA), and survivor tax brackets all intersect. A strategy that looks harmless at age 40 can become very expensive at age 72.

In this chapter, we are going to expose the most common tech strategies sold as solutions, but that often function as slow leaks in your financial bucket. Some of these strategies are not always wrong. In rare situations, they may even be appropriate. But for most couples in the 55 to 75 age range, they are either unnecessary, inefficient, or outright harmful.

Think of this chapter as defensive driving for your tax life. Before we accelerate into advanced strategies – Roth conversions, brokerage optimization, Social Security planning – we need to be clear of the road hazards. **Sometimes the fastest way to build wealth isn't finding a new tactic. It's stopping the wrong one.**

Five strategies are commonly promoted as tax smart – especially to high-income earners and pre-retirees – but often do more harm than good when implemented mindlessly. In this chapter, will examine:

1. Tax-deferral only
2. Permanent life insurance
3. Non-qualified annuities
4. Municipal bonds

Let's get started.

Tax Deferral Only

If you have been a diligent saver for the past 30 years, there's a very good chance that most – or even all – of your retirement savings, traditional 401(k)s, and IRAs. You did what you are told: max out the 401(k), take the deduction, lower your taxable income, and get a bigger refund. Year after year, it felt responsible and productive. In many cases, it was. The problem is not tax-deferral itself. The problem is tax deferral *only*.

The Hidden Assumption

Every time you contributed pre-tax dollars to a traditional 401(k) or deducted a traditional IRA contribution, you made a bet that your tax rate in retirement would be lower than it is today. Sometimes that bet wins. But many couples over 50 discover – too late – that they never actually evaluated the bet. They kept deferring because that's what their CPA recommended each March during their annual tax return review.

Here's the uncomfortable truth: most tax preparers are paid to look backward, not forward. If your CPA can reduce last year's taxable income by $20,000 and increase your refund, that feels like a victory. You are happy, they're happy, and you come back next year. But that $20,000 didn't disappear; it moved into an account that will eventually be taxed, often at higher tax rates, whether you need the money or not. Rarely does anyone stop to model what your tax rate might be when that bill finally comes due.

The RMD Time Bomb

Traditional retirement accounts are not tax-free; they are tax postponed. Beginning at age 73 (and age 75 for folks born on or after 1960), the IRS forces you to start taking Required Minimum Distributions (RMDs). You don't get to decide whether you want the income, and you don't get to leave it alone, simply because your Social Security and pension already cover your lifestyle. The government decides, and every dollar distributed is taxed at ordinary income.

Consider Bob and Sue from our case study. Between Social Security and pensions, they already have $100,000 of income. If Bob has $600,000 in his TSP and Sue has $200,000 in her 403B, they combined RMD could easily add another three30,000 to 40,000 $ of forced income in t that additional income can cause more of their Social Security to become taxable, push them over and IRMAA threshold and increased Medicare premiums, two years later, and create a larger tax burden for the surviving spouse who will file as single. Their heirs may inherit sizable pretax accounts and be forced to empty them within 10 years at their own, often higher, tax rates. All of this stems from decades of a simple, unquestioned strategy: defer, defer, defer.

The Refund Illusion

There is something psychologically powerful about a tax refund. It feels like found money and serves us proof that you "did it right." But a refund is not a bonus; it is simply your own money returned to you. Maximizing a refund by maximizing the deferrals can create a dangerous illusion of progress. If you reduce your taxes by $5000 each year through additional pre-tax contributions, that sounds fantastic. However, if those contributions grow for 20 years and or later withdrawn at higher tax rates – triggering IRA, increasing Social Security, taxation, and compressing tax brackets for the surviving spouse – that earlier "savings" may ultimately cost far more than they saved. Tax deferral feels like winning because the benefit is immediate and invisible, while the cost is delayed and hidden.

When Tax Deferral Makes Sense

To be clear, traditional accounts are not inherently bad. For high earners in peak tax brackets, strategic deferral can be extremely valuable. For couples planning large Roth conversions in early retirement, pretax balances may be part of a thoughtful long-term plan. The mistake is not using tax deferral; the mistake is using it exclusively without modeling future income, RMDs, Social Security taxation, Medicare, premiums, and Survivor tax brackets.

A healthy tax strategy creates flexibility across multiple buckets: some money is taxable, some is tax-deferred, and some is tax-free. When all your assets sit in one bucket, you don't have a coordinated strategy – you have a tax problem, waiting for age 73. Unfortunately, by the time most couples recognize the concentration risk, the runway to address it is much shorter than it was.

The good news is that the time bomb is not untouchable. In Chapter 4, we will walk through how strategically diffuse it using Roth contributions and Roth conversions, intentionally filling low tax brackets before RMDs begin, and creating tax-free income that restores flexibility later in life. Tax deferral created the imbalance; thoughtful tax diversification can correct it. But first we need to exam the other strategies that often compound the problem rather than solve it.

Permanent Life Insurance

Permanent life insurance is often positioned as the sophisticated, tax-advantaged solution for high-income earners who "make too much" to contribute directly to a Roth IRA. The pitch typically sounds something like this: grow money tax-deferred, access it tax-free through policy loans, avoid market volatility, and leave behind a tax-free death benefit. On the surface, it can sound like a financial Swiss Army knife—insurance, investment, and tax strategy wrapped into one tidy package.

To understand the appeal, we need to understand how the policy actually works. With permanent life insurance (whole life, universal life, indexed universal life), you pay a premium. Part of that premium goes toward the cost of insurance—the death benefit—and part goes into a cash value account within the policy. The cash value grows tax-deferred, and over time, it may accumulate enough to support withdrawals.

Accessing the money is where the "tax-free income" narrative begins. Sales representatives explain that you can take partial surrenders up to your basis (the amount you've paid in) tax-free, and then access additional funds through policy loans. Because loans are not taxable events, the income can be structured to appear tax-free. In retirement illustrations, it often appears as a private pension stream with no tax due.

But as with many tax strategies, the illustration highlights the benefit and soft-pedals the cost.

Problem #1: Low Long-Term Returns and Heavy Early Costs

The first issue is performance. Cash value policies typically take 10–20 years to break even due to front-loaded commissions, mortality costs, and internal policy expenses. In many policies, 80–95% of your first-year premium goes toward fees and commissions rather than cash value accumulation. After the long climb to break-even, the long-term internal rate of return on the cash value is often in the 3–5% range.

Let's compare that to a simple alternative. Suppose you saved $1,000 per month for 30 years. If that money compounds at 4% annually inside a cash value policy, you would accumulate approximately $694,000. That's on $360,000 of total contributions. Now, assume you invested the same $1,000 per month in a diversified equity mutual fund portfolio that earns 10% gross annually. Even after paying 15% in capital gains and dividend taxes every year along the way, your net return might reasonably be around 8.5%. Over 30 years, at 8.5%, that same savings rate grows to roughly $1.65 million.

That is more than double the ending value, and certainly more than the death benefit would be. And if you have been paying taxes every year, that end value would be largely tax-free. (Alternatively, we could use a higher net annual return and pay taxes at the end, but the result would be even higher.)

Even after paying taxes each year in the non-qualified account, you end up with substantially more after-tax wealth. Remember the goal from Chapter 1: not to pay the least taxes, but to have the most money after taxes. I would rather pay taxes on growth that compounds at 8.5% than avoid taxes on growth that compounds at 4%.

Insurance representatives will often counter that the stock market is risky and that you could lose 30–40% in a downturn. That is true in the short term. But you are virtually guaranteed to lose a significant portion of your first year's premium to policy fees, and you are virtually guaranteed to wait a decade or more to break even. A temporary market decline is volatility; a decade-long climb out of fees is structural drag. In many cases, that drag is the greater risk.

Problem #2: Policy Loans Aren't Unique

The second issue is the supposed uniqueness of policy loans. Yes, loans are not taxable events. But you can borrow against many types of assets tax-free. You can borrow against your home with a home equity line of credit. You can borrow against a brokerage account using a securities-backed line of credit. In each case, the loan itself is not income.

With life insurance, you are borrowing against your own cash value and paying interest to the insurance company to use money that is already yours. If the loan is not managed carefully, interest can compound and erode both the cash value and the death benefit. The "tax-free income" is not free; it is debt secured by your policy.

Problem #3: Ordinary Income on Surrender

The third issue appears if you ever decide the policy no longer fits your plan. If you surrender a permanent life insurance policy with cash value greater than your basis (the premiums you've paid), the gain is taxed as ordinary income—not capital gains. After years of low returns and high fees, you may still owe ordinary income tax on the growth if you exit the policy.

For most couples in the 55–75 age range, permanent life insurance as an accumulation vehicle is simply an expensive way to chase tax deferral. Most are better served by directing after-tax dollars into Roth accounts (which we'll cover in Chapter 4) or diversified nonqualified brokerage accounts (Chapter 5). Both provide flexibility, transparency, and—most importantly—a higher probability of maximizing long-term, after-tax wealth.

It is also important to understand the incentive structure behind many of these recommendations. Permanent life insurance policies often pay commissions of 50–100% of the first year's premium to the selling agent. In our example of $1,000 per month, that is $12,000 per year in premiums—meaning the agent may receive $6,000 to $12,000 upfront for implementing the policy. When compensation is structured this way, it should not surprise us that the upside is emphasized and the structural drag of fees, low returns, and long break-even periods is minimized or glossed over.

This does not mean every insurance professional is acting in bad faith. But it does mean you should ask hard questions and follow the incentives. When someone earns more from one strategy than another, that difference matters. If you would like a deeper dive into how these policies are designed, illustrated, and sold—along with a more detailed breakdown of their internal costs—I have several videos walking through real examples on my YouTube channel: YouTube.com/@FreemanLinde.

Non-Qualified Annuities

Nonqualified annuities are often marketed as tax-efficient accumulation vehicles for investors who have already maxed out their retirement accounts. The pitch is straightforward: invest after-tax dollars, allow the money to grow tax-deferred inside the annuity, and delay paying taxes until you withdraw the funds in the future. On the surface, that sounds attractive—especially to investors frustrated by annual 1099s reporting interest, dividends, and capital gains.

Here is how they work. You contribute after-tax money into the annuity contract. The investments inside the annuity grow tax-deferred, meaning you do not receive annual tax reporting on gains. However, when you take withdrawals, the tax is calculated under LIFO (last in, first out), meaning the gains are withdrawn first and taxed as ordinary income. If you withdraw before age 59½, you may also owe a 10% penalty on the taxable portion, similar to retirement accounts. In addition, many annuities carry surrender periods of 7–10 years, during which withdrawals above a small free-withdrawal amount trigger surrender charges.

At first glance, tax deferral appears to be the primary benefit. But as we've seen before, deferral alone is not the goal. Let's examine the trade-offs.

Problem #1: High Fees

Many variable annuities carry a Mortality and Expense (M&E) charge of around 1.3% annually. Add administrative fees and the higher internal expenses of subaccount mutual funds, and total annual costs typically range from 2% to 4%. That is a significant hurdle to overcome before you even begin compounding.

You are effectively paying 2–4% per year to defer today's capital gains into the future. That is an expensive trade. If your underlying portfolio might reasonably earn 8–10% gross over time, losing several percentage points annually to fees dramatically reduces long-term growth. Remember, we want more money after taxes—not fewer taxes on a much smaller pile.

Problem #2: Surrender Periods and Liquidity Constraints

Annuities often lock up your money for 7–10 years with surrender schedules that penalize withdrawals beyond a modest annual allowance. During that time, if your circumstances change—such as your health, family needs, or business opportunities—accessing your own capital can be costly. On top of that, the 59½ rule applies to the taxable portion of withdrawals, meaning early access can trigger both ordinary income taxes and a 10% penalty.

Flexibility has value. When you sacrifice liquidity for tax deferral, you should demand a meaningful long-term benefit in exchange. In many cases, the benefit does not justify the constraint.

Problem #3: Converting Capital Gains into Ordinary Income

This is perhaps the most overlooked issue. In a standard non-qualified brokerage account, long-term capital gains and qualified dividends are taxed at preferential rates—generally 0%, 15%, or 20% depending on taxable income, as we covered in Chapter 2. Those gains stack on top of ordinary income and are often taxed at lower rates than wages or IRA withdrawals.

Inside a non-qualified annuity, however, all gains are eventually taxed as ordinary income when withdrawn. In other words, you are deferring capital gains rates of 0–15% today only to potentially pay ordinary income rates of 12–32% (or higher) in the future. That is not tax arbitrage; it is tax rate conversion in the wrong direction.

You have turned one of the most favorable tax treatments in the code—long-term capital gains—into one of the least favorable.

Problem #4: No Step-Up in Basis

One of the major advantages of taxable brokerage accounts is the step-up in basis at death. If you purchase an investment for $100,000 and it grows to $400,000, your heirs receive a new basis of $400,000 upon your death. If they sell immediately, there is no capital gains tax owed on that $300,000 of appreciation.

Non-qualified annuities do not receive the same treatment. While the contract value may transfer to beneficiaries, the gain portion is still taxable as ordinary income when distributed. Your heirs do not receive a step-up that eliminates the deferred gain. Instead, the tax deferral you enjoyed during life may become an ordinary income tax burden for them.

Once again, a feature that sounds beneficial—tax deferral—can quietly undermine long-term, multi-generational tax efficiency.

As with permanent life insurance, compensation structures matter. Annuities often pay commissions ranging from 7% to 12% of the amount invested. On a $300,000 contribution, that could mean $21,000 to $36,000 paid to the selling representative. When thousands of dollars are at stake up front, it is not surprising that the tax-deferral story is highlighted while the high fees, surrender schedules, ordinary-income treatment, and lack of a step-up are downplayed.

To be clear, annuities can have appropriate uses in certain limited circumstances, particularly when income guarantees are the primary objective. But as tax-efficient accumulation vehicles, non-qualified annuities often trade liquidity, lower capital gains rates, and long-term growth for the expense of deferral. The tax benefits can just as easily become tax drawbacks, and once again, the result may be less wealth after taxes rather than more.

Municipal Bonds

Municipal bonds are debt issued by states and local governments. In exchange for lending them money, you receive interest payments that are generally exempt from federal income tax and, if you own bonds issued in your home state, often exempt from state income tax as well. Because of this feature, municipal bonds are frequently described as "tax-free income" investments.

That sounds attractive, particularly for retirees trying to manage taxable income. But as with every strategy in this chapter, we must ask the right question: does it produce the most money after taxes, or simply the least taxes?

Let's use a real-world comparison. As of this writing, Vanguard's Tax-Exempt Bond Index Fund (VTEAX) yields 3.29%, while Vanguard's Total Bond Market Index Fund (VBTLX) yields 4.19%. Municipal bond income is federally tax-free; taxable bond income is not.

To determine which is better, we calculate the taxable-equivalent yield. In other words, what tax bracket would make a 4.19% taxable yield equivalent to 3.29% tax-free? The formula is:

Taxable-equivalent yield = Municipal yield ÷ (1 − tax rate).

Setting the two equal:

$3.29\% \div (1 - t) = 4.19\%$

Solving for t gives approximately 21.5%. In practical terms, you need to be in roughly the 22% federal tax bracket or higher before the tax-free 3.29% yield becomes more attractive than the 4.19% taxable yield on an after-tax basis. If you are in the 12% bracket, the taxable bond's after-tax yield (4.19% × 0.88 = 3.69%) would still exceed the municipal bond's 3.29%.

Now, there are legitimate scenarios where municipal bonds can make sense even at somewhat lower brackets. For example, reducing Adjusted Gross Income may help manage Social Security taxation, avoid crossing an IRMAA threshold, or reduce exposure to other income-based phaseouts we discussed in Chapter 2. In those situations, the indirect tax effects may tilt the balance.

Our criticism is not that municipal bonds are inherently flawed. The issue is their automatic use simply because the income is labeled "tax-free." Tax-free income is not automatically superior if it produces a lower after-tax yield. Once again, the goal is not minimizing taxes in isolation. The goal is maximizing lifetime, after-tax wealth.

The "Tax-Free" Retirement

In recent years, several books, seminars, and online personalities have promoted the idea of achieving a completely tax-free retirement. The pitch is simple and emotionally compelling: structure your savings so you pay no taxes once you stop working. The strategies often emphasize heavy use of Roth accounts, Roth conversions, and insurance-based products marketed as tax-free income vehicles.

At first glance, this sounds like the ultimate win. Who wouldn't want to retire and owe nothing to the IRS? But once again, we must return to the core question: does paying zero taxes in retirement maximize lifetime, after-tax wealth—or does it simply shift taxes to a different phase of life?

For many high earners, the "tax-free retirement" approach means paying 22% or higher marginal tax rates today to avoid paying 10% or 12% later. In other words, you willingly prepay taxes at elevated working-year brackets to avoid filling lower brackets in retirement. That is not tax optimization; it is bracket mismanagement.

This strategy is the mirror image of the Tax-Deferral-Only mistake. Instead of deferring everything and creating an RMD time bomb, you accelerate everything—paying as much tax as possible during peak earning years. In both cases, the problem is extremism. You are either overusing deferral or overusing tax-free accumulation, and in both scenarios, you risk ending up with less overall wealth.

A great tax strategy does not avoid low tax brackets—it intentionally uses them. The 10% and 12% brackets are gifts in the tax code. The goal is often to earn income in higher brackets while working and then strategically fill lower brackets in retirement through thoughtful withdrawals or conversions. If you are currently in the 22%+ bracket, designing your entire plan around achieving a 0% retirement bracket usually means you have prepaid too much tax too soon.

To be clear, there are situations where a 0% retirement bracket can occur naturally and intelligently. A couple who spend decades in the 12% bracket while working may build Roth assets and modest traditional balances, allowing them to remain at or near 0% in retirement without sacrificing growth. But that is very different from a high-income household aggressively prepaying taxes at elevated rates to pursue a headline goal.

Too often, the "tax-free retirement" movement also leans heavily on permanent life insurance or other complex products to achieve that outcome. As we've already discussed, layering high fees and modest returns into the strategy can undermine the very wealth you are trying to protect.

Zero taxes is not the objective. Smart use of tax brackets is. When you focus on filling the right brackets at the right time—rather than eliminating taxes entirely—you give yourself the highest probability of ending up with more money after taxes over your lifetime.

Conclusion: Beware of the Tax Label

Each strategy in this chapter shares a common marketing hook: tax savings. Tax-deferred. Tax-free. Tax-advantaged. Even the promise of a completely "tax-free retirement." Those labels are powerful because they appeal to something we all feel—the desire to keep more of what we earn. But as we established in Chapter 1, reducing taxes and increasing wealth are not the same thing.

Tax-deferral-only strategies can create RMD time bombs. Permanent life insurance can suppress long-term growth in exchange for expensive deferral. Nonqualified annuities can convert favorable capital gains into higher-taxed ordinary income while imposing substantial fees and surrender restrictions. Municipal bonds can produce lower after-tax yields simply because the word "tax-free" feels comforting. And the pursuit of a zero-percent retirement bracket can cause high earners to prepay taxes at 22% or higher today to avoid filling 10% and 12% brackets later.

In every case, the danger is isolation. When a strategy is evaluated only on how much tax it saves this year—or how little tax appears on a 1099—we risk ignoring growth, flexibility, liquidity, bracket management, and long-term estate consequences. Taxes matter, but taxes are only one variable in the equation.

The right tax strategy is rarely about eliminating taxes. It is about coordinating tax buckets, investment returns, income timing, bracket management, and estate considerations to improve your lifetime and legacy outcomes. Sometimes that will mean deferring taxes. Sometimes it will mean intentionally paying them at lower rates. Sometimes it will mean accepting a little more current taxation in exchange for significantly greater long-term compounding.

The families who win are not those who chase the lowest tax bill each April or aim for a headline of "zero taxes in retirement." They are the ones who build a plan that integrates taxes into a broader strategy for growth and flexibility.

Now that we've cleared away the most common tax-saving mistakes, it's time to turn toward proactive strategies that can actually increase your after-tax wealth. In the next chapter, we'll address one of the most powerful tools available for defusing the tax-deferral time bomb and properly using lower brackets: Roth contributions and Roth conversions.

Chapter Summary
- The goal of tax planning is not to pay the least amount of taxes, but to maximize lifetime, after-tax wealth.
- Tax deferral alone can create future problems, particularly through Required Minimum Distributions (RMDs), Social Security taxation, IRMAA surcharges, and compressed survivor tax brackets.
- Permanent life insurance policies often carry high early costs, modest long-term returns, and commission-driven incentives that can reduce long-term wealth despite tax-deferred growth.
- Non-qualified annuities frequently impose 2–4% annual fees on top of surrender restrictions, convert favorable capital gains treatment into ordinary income taxation, and eliminate step-up in basis advantages.
- Municipal bonds provide tax-free income, but may produce lower after-tax yields depending on your tax bracket and overall planning situation.
- Pursuing a "tax-free retirement" can lead high earners to prepay taxes at 22%+ today to avoid filling lower 10% and 12% brackets later, which may reduce overall lifetime wealth.

- Labels such as "tax-free" and "tax-deferred" are not synonymous with "wealth-maximizing." A strong strategy intentionally uses low tax brackets rather than avoiding them.

Action Items

1. Review Your Account Allocation. List the balances in your taxable, tax-deferred, and tax-free accounts. Are you overly concentrated in one bucket—either all pre-tax or all Roth?
2. Evaluate Your Marginal Bracket Today. Identify your current marginal tax rate and compare it to realistic projections of your retirement brackets. Are you deferring income mindlessly, or prepaying taxes unnecessarily?
3. Evaluate Existing Insurance Policies. If you own a permanent life insurance policy, request an in-force illustration showing projected returns and break-even timing. Compare the internal rate of return to reasonable long-term market expectations.
4. Analyze Any Annuity Contracts. Identify total annual fees, surrender periods, and how withdrawals are taxed. Ask whether the tax deferral justifies the cost, loss of capital gains treatment, and lack of step-up in basis.
5. Compare Bond Yields Properly. If you hold municipal bonds, calculate the taxable-equivalent yield based on your marginal bracket. Confirm that the tax-free income actually produces a superior after-tax result.
6. Plan to Use, Not Waste, Low Brackets. Consider whether your plan allows you to intentionally fill lower tax brackets

in retirement rather than avoiding them entirely. Aiming for zero taxes is rarely the optimal objective.

Taking these steps does not mean you must unwind every product immediately. It means you are evaluating each strategy according to the right objective: maximizing the amount of money you and your family keep after taxes over your lifetime.

Part 2 – Tax Strategies

To Roth or Not To Roth

Chapter 4

Traditional vs. Roth is the Question

This chapter will tackle one of the most important and misunderstood questions in retirement and tax planning:

Should you contribute to Traditional accounts, Roth accounts, or both? And when does a Roth conversion make sense?

For couples over fifty, this decision can mean the difference between paying taxes at 12% or 32%, avoiding or triggering IRMAA, and leaving a tax burden—or a tax gift—to your children.

Before we dive in, here is the roadmap for this chapter:

Roth vs. Traditional Recap. A quick overview of the difference between Traditional and Roth accounts, contributions, and conversions—especially helpful if you skimmed Chapter 2.

Strategic Decision Framework. A practical system for deciding whether you should make Traditional or Roth contributions and whether Roth conversions make sense in your situation.

Advanced Tax Planning. The additional phaseouts, thresholds, stacking rules, and hidden brackets that affect retirement taxation far beyond the standard marginal tax rates.

The RMD Time Bomb. How Required Minimum Distributions are calculated, why they can explode your tax return in your seventies, and how they silently impact Medicare premiums and Social Security taxation.

The Roth Timelines. The different phases for Roth contributions and conversions—from peak earning years to early retirement, to the RMD years—and how strategy shifts over time.

We'll wrap up with a strong encouragement: projecting and calculating Roth strategies without modeling the long-term tax impact is guesswork. These decisions deserve intentional forecasting.

As always, remember the goal from Chapter 1:

The goal is not to pay the least amount of taxes. The goal is to maximize the amount of money you have after taxes over your lifetime.

Throughout this chapter, we'll apply the concepts to Steve & Rachel, Chuck & Diane, and Bob & Sue to show how income level, age, and account structure affect the decision to contribute or convert to a Roth.

Let's begin with a quick recap.

Roth vs. Traditional Recap

Before we build a strategy, we need clarity.

At their core, Traditional and Roth retirement accounts are mirror images of each other. The difference is not whether you pay taxes. It is when you pay them.

How Traditional Accounts Work

Traditional retirement accounts include Traditional 401(k)s, 403(b)s, 457 plans, SIMPLE IRAs, and deductible Traditional IRAs.

They follow this structure:

- **Contributions:** Pre-tax (or tax-deductible). You receive a deduction today.
- **Growth:** Tax-deferred. No annual taxation on interest, dividends, or gains.
- **Distributions:** 100% taxable as ordinary income.

In simple terms: **No tax now. Tax later.**

Traditional accounts lower your taxable income today, but every dollar coming out in retirement is added to your tax return.

How Roth Accounts Work

Roth accounts include Roth 401(k)s and Roth IRAs.
They follow this structure:

- **Contributions:** Post-tax. No deduction today.
- **Growth:** Tax-deferred.
- **Distributions:** 100% tax-free if rules are followed.

In simple terms: **Tax now. No tax later.**
You voluntarily pay taxes on the seed, so the harvest is tax-free.
Remember the Roth Distribution Ordering Rules and 5-Year Clocks from Chapter Two.

Contributions vs. Conversions

Many people confuse these two terms. They are not the same.

Contributions

A **contribution** is new money going into a retirement account from earned income.

For 2026 (Married Filing Jointly):

- **401(k), 403(b), and most 457 plan elective deferral limit:** $24,500 per person
- **Catch-up contribution (age 50+):** $8,000 per person
  → Total possible per person age 50+: **$32,500**

(SECURE 2.0 also created a higher catch-up limit for ages 60–63. For 2026, that higher catch-up amount is $11,250 instead of $8,000. If you are in that age window, your plan may allow a higher contribution.)

IRA contribution limits for 2026 (Traditional + Roth combined, per person):

- **$7,500 per person**
- **$1,100 catch-up (age 50+)**
  → Total possible per person age 50+: **$8,600**

However, IRA contributions are subject to income phaseouts. For Roth IRA contributions in 2026 (MFJ):

- Ability to contribute begins phasing out at **$242,000 of Modified Adjusted Gross Income (MAGI)**
- Fully phased out at **$252,000 MAGI**

For deductible Traditional IRA contributions (when covered by a retirement plan at work), deductibility phases out between **$129,000 and $149,000 MAGI (MFJ)** (when the spouse making the contribution is covered by a workplace retirement plan). The Bonus Material includes a flowchart that makes it easy to determine if you can make a deductible IRA contribution or not.

Important requirements for contributions:

- You must have **earned income**.
- You must stay within the income limits for Roth IRA eligibility.
- Employer plans (401(k)s) do **not** have income limits for Roth vs. Traditional contributions.

A contribution is limited. It is capped each year.

Conversions

A **Roth conversion** is when you move money from a Traditional (pre-tax) retirement account into a Roth account. You are not adding new money. You are changing the tax character of existing money.

Key differences from contributions:

- There is **no income limit** to do a Roth conversion.
- There is **no annual dollar cap** on how much you can convert.
- You do **not** need earned income.

However:

- The amount converted is added to your taxable income for that year.
- It is taxed as ordinary income.
- Ideally, taxes should be paid from outside funds (not from the IRA itself).

If a couple converts $100,000 from a Traditional IRA to a Roth IRA in 2026, that $100,000 is added to their taxable income and taxed at their marginal rate (plus any IRMAA or other impacts).

In summary:

- **Contribution = new earned money going in. Limited.**
- **Conversion = existing pre-tax money moved to Roth. Unlimited, but taxable.**

Understanding this difference is critical. Contributions are about where you save. Conversions are about when you choose to pay taxes.

A Critical Warning About Paying Conversion Taxes

Here is a mistake I see regularly. If you are under 59½ and you do a Roth conversion, you will owe income taxes on the amount converted. If you withhold those taxes **from the IRA itself**, that withheld amount is considered a distribution.

And if you are under 59½, that distribution:

- Is subject to a **10% penalty**, and
- Permanently reduces the amount you are converting into tax-free growth.

Example: Steve (age 54) converts $100,000 from a Traditional IRA to a Roth IRA. He owes $24,000 in federal taxes. Instead of paying from savings, he withholds the $24,000 from the IRA.

Result:

- $100,000 is taxable income.
- $24,000 is treated as an early distribution.
- He will owe an additional $2,400 penalty at tax time (10% of $24,000, plus State Penalties).
- The conversion results in a 26.4% tax rate.
- Only $76,000 ends up in the Roth.

That is expensive. The general best practice: If you are under 59½, always pay conversion taxes from outside funds.

Once you understand these distribution mechanics, the Roth strategy becomes far more precise. Roths are powerful—but only when used intentionally.

Now that we understand how the tools work, let's move to the real question: how do you decide which one to use?

2. Strategic Decision Framework

At its simplest level, the Roth decision comes down to one principle: You can pay taxes now or later. The goal is to pay them at the lowest possible rate.

That's it.

Every Traditional contribution is a decision to pay taxes later. Every Roth contribution or conversion is a decision to pay taxes now. The only variable that truly matters is this:

Will your tax rate be higher or lower in the future than it is today?

To make the math simple, let's assume your combined federal and state marginal tax rate today is **25%**. (Not a bracket—just an illustrative blended rate.)

We'll compare three scenarios per $1,000 of income.

To keep the math clean, assume the investment ultimately **doubles** before distribution. The growth rate and time period do not matter. If both accounts grow at the same rate, they double at the same point. The only difference is taxation.

Scenario 1: Same Tax Rate Later (25% Now, 25% Later)

	Traditional	**Roth**
Initial Income	$1,000	$1,000
Tax Today (25%)	$0	$250
Amount Invested	$1,000	$750
Value After Doubling	$2,000	$1,500
Tax at Distribution (25%)	$500	$0
Final After-Tax Amount	$1,500	$1,500

When tax rates are identical, the outcome is identical.

Scenario 2: Higher Tax Rate Later (25% Now, 28% Later)

	Traditional	Roth
Initial Income	$1,000	$1,000
Tax Today (25%)	$0	$250
Amount Invested	$1,000	$750
Value After Doubling	$2,000	$1,500
Tax at Distribution (28%)	$560	$0
Final After-Tax Amount	$1,440	$1,500

Here, Roth wins because you paid 25% instead of 28%.

Scenario 3: Lower Tax Rate Later (25% Now, 22% Later)

	Traditional	Roth
Initial Income	$1,000	$1,000
Tax Today (25%)	$0	$250
Amount Invested	$1,000	$750
Value After Doubling	$2,000	$1,500

	Traditional	Roth
Tax at Distribution (22%)	$440	$0
Final After-Tax Amount	$1,560	$1,500

Here, Traditional wins because you deferred taxes from 25% to 22%.

"It's Only 3%... That's Not Much"

A 3% difference per $1,000 is only $30. Or if comparing 25% to 28%, it's $30 more per $1,000. That doesn't sound life-changing. But retirement isn't one $1,000 withdrawal.

Let's assume you withdraw **$50,000 per year**, and those withdrawals increase with inflation at **3% annually** for 30+ years. The total withdrawals over 30 years would equal approximately **$2.4 Million.**

Now apply a 3% tax difference to that lifetime income stream: $2,400,000 × 3% ≈ **$72,000**

That's over $70,000 in extra lifetime taxes—simply from being in a tax bracket that is 3% higher.

And this example assumes a modest retirement income. Many couples will withdraw more than $50,000 per year. Small percentage differences compound into large dollar differences.

The Real Question

The Roth vs. Traditional decision is not about guessing whether taxes will "go up in the future" politically.

It is about projecting **your future personal tax rate**.

- Will you have large Required Minimum Distributions?
- Will Social Security be taxable?
- Will you trigger IRMAA?
- Will one spouse die and push the survivor into single tax brackets?

Your future tax rate is determined far more by your balance sheet than by Congress.

So the framework becomes:

- Identify your current marginal effective tax rate.
- Project your likely retirement tax rate.
- Pay taxes in the lower of the two periods.

Now we need to explore what actually drives those future rates—because retirement taxation is rarely as simple as just looking at the tax brackets.

3. Advanced Tax Planning

Up to this point, we have simplified the decision to one variable: your tax rate now versus your tax rate later.

So let's start with the obvious place—federal tax brackets.

2026 Federal Tax Brackets (Married Filing Jointly)

For 2026, the official federal tax brackets for MFJ are:

- **10%** – $0 to $24,800
- **12%** – $24,801 to $100,800
- **22%** – $100,801 to $211,400
- **24%** – $211,401 to $403,550
- **32%** – $403,551 to $512,450

- **35%** – $512,451 to $768,700
- **37%** – Over $768,700

The **2026 Standard Deduction for Married Filing Jointly is $32,200.**

Since tax brackets are based on Taxable Income, and Taxable Income = AGI minus deductions, we can estimate the AGI where each bracket effectively begins by adding back the standard deduction.

Advanced Tax Brackets by AGI for MFJ in 2026

(Numbers marked with a * are based on Taxable Income + adding back in the $32,200 standard deduction. Your actual threshold will be based on Taxable Income, not these AGI numbers. ** is based on MAGI, which is likely close to or the same as AGI.)

- **$32,200** – Start of the 10% Bracket*
- **$57,000** – Start of the 12% Bracket*
- **$133,000** – Start of the 22% Bracket*
- **$150,000** – Start: Senior Bonus Deduction Phase-Out
- **$200,000** – End: Senior Bonus Deduction Phase-Out
- **$218,000** – **IRMAA Threshold 1****
- **$243,600** – Start of the 24% Tax Bracket*
- **$250,000** – 3.8% Net Investment Income Tax**
- **$274,000** – IRMAA Threshold 2**
- **$326,000** – IRMAA Threshold 3**
- **$390,000** – IRMAA Threshold 4**
- **$435,750** – Start of the 32% Tax Bracket*
- **$544,650** – Start of the 35% Tax Bracket*
- **$750,000** – Highest IRMAA Tier**
- **$800,900*** – Start of the 37% Tax Bracket

Notice how many things begin to stack up between roughly $130,000 and $300,000 in income.

A couple can be sitting comfortably in the 22% federal bracket and simultaneously:

- Losing part of their senior deduction
- Triggering IRMAA surcharges
- Activating the 3.8% NIIT
- Increasing the taxable portion of Social Security

That is where the analysis becomes more complicated.

Why This Matters

Notice something important:

- Federal tax brackets are based on **Taxable Income**.
- IRMAA and NIIT are based on **MAGI**.
- Social Security taxation depends on **Provisional Income**.

Three different definitions of income. This means your "true" marginal effective rate may not be 22%. It might be:

- 22% federal
- 3.8% NIIT
- IRMAA premium increases
- Increased taxation of Social Security

A 22% decision on paper could functionally be 30% or more. And this is before we even discuss Required Minimum Distributions.

Now we need to address the biggest hidden driver of future tax rates—the RMD time bomb.

4. The RMD Time Bomb

At some point, the IRS stops waiting. If you have money in Traditional retirement accounts, the government will eventually require you to take money out—and pay taxes on it—whether you need the income or not. These mandatory withdrawals are called **Required Minimum Distributions (RMDs)**, and for many retirees, they become the single largest driver of unexpected tax increases.

How RMDs Are Calculated

RMDs currently begin at age 73 (and later at age 75 for younger cohorts under current law). Each year's RMD is calculated using a straightforward formula:

Prior Year December 31 Account Balance ÷ IRS Life Expectancy Factor

The IRS provides a **Uniform Lifetime Table** that determines your required payout percentage. At age 73, the divisor is 26.5 (roughly 3.77%), at age 80, it is 20.2 (roughly 4.95%), and by age 85, it falls to 16.0 (6.25%). As you age, the percentage increases, meaning a larger portion of your account must be withdrawn each year, regardless of market conditions.

To simplify this, I've included an **RMD Payout Percentage Table** in the Book Bonus materials so you can quickly look up your required withdrawal percentage. For example, if Bob has $1,000,000 in his Traditional IRA at age 73, his RMD would be $1,000,000 ÷ 26.5 = $37,736. That $37,736 is fully taxable as ordinary income, and if his portfolio grows, next year's required distribution will likely be even larger.

Important RMD Rules for Conversions

There are two critical rules that many retirees misunderstand. First, you must take your RMD before doing a Roth conversion in any year that you are subject to RMDs. Second, an RMD itself cannot be converted to a Roth. If you are required to take a $40,000 RMD, that $40,000 must be distributed and taxed; only amounts above that can be converted.

This sequencing requirement is one reason waiting until your seventies to "start doing Roth conversions" is often too late. The RMD hits first, increasing your taxable income before you have the opportunity to manage the bracket intentionally.

What If You Don't Need the RMD?

Many retirees respond by saying they will reinvest the RMD in a brokerage account. That is perfectly allowable, but it creates a second-order tax effect. Once those dollars are in a non-qualified account, the interest becomes annually taxable as ordinary income, dividends increase taxable income each year, and capital gains are eventually realized and taxed.

As a result, your AGI remains elevated, NIIT exposure may increase, IRMAA thresholds may be triggered or sustained, and a larger portion of Social Security may remain taxable. The money does not disappear—it simply changes tax buckets—and the tax stacking problem often continues for the rest of your life.

How RMDs Trigger Threshold Stacking

Because RMDs are added directly to your AGI, they can push you into a higher federal tax bracket while simultaneously activating other thresholds. A larger RMD can trigger IRMAA surcharges, activate the 3.8% NIIT, increase the taxable portion of Social Security, and phase out deductions and credits. What looked manageable in your early retirement years can become far more complex once RMDs begin.

It is not uncommon for a couple who lived comfortably in the 12% bracket during their sixties to find themselves back in the 22% bracket in their mid-seventies—not because they increased spending, but because they saved diligently. The better you save, the larger your potential RMD problem can become, especially if you have pensions, Social Security, and substantial pre-tax balances.

Three Ways to Control RMDs

You cannot eliminate RMDs from Traditional accounts once they begin, but you can influence their long-term impact.

1. Spend More

RMDs are less disruptive for retirees who are already spending the money for lifestyle needs. The largest RMD challenges typically fall to disciplined savers with substantial portfolios, who live below their means and intend to leave large legacy assets. If the money is ultimately going to heirs anyway, it may be more tax-efficient to shift some of it to Roth earlier rather than allow RMDs to compound the problem later.

2. Qualified Charitable Distributions (QCDs)

Beginning at age 70½, you can direct up to $100,000 per year (indexed for inflation) directly from an IRA to qualified charities. These distributions count toward your RMD but do not increase your AGI, which means they avoid triggering IRMAA or NIIT and do not increase Social Security taxation. For charitably inclined households, QCDs are one of the most powerful RMD management tools available, and we will cover them in detail in Chapter 7.

3. Proactive Roth Conversions Before RMD Age

The most strategic way to control future RMDs is to reduce the size of the Traditional account before RMDs begin. Converting portions of your IRA in your sixties—or in the gap years between retirement and age 73—can lower future RMDs, flatten lifetime tax brackets, reduce IRMAA exposure later, and create tax-free legacy assets for heirs. Roth conversion planning is often most powerful in early retirement, when income is temporarily lower and before mandatory distributions begin, accelerating the tax burden.

RMDs are not merely a distribution rule; they are a tax accelerant. Now that we understand how they work and how they compound other thresholds, we can explore when conversions make the most sense across different life phases.

5. The Roth Timelines

Roth strategy is not a single decision—it is a series of decisions made across different phases of life. These phases are not perfectly sequential. They depend on when you retire, the age gap between spouses, when Social Security is claimed, and when Medicare begins. Most couples will experience three to five of these phases, not all eight.

The key is understanding what tax forces are active in each window and how they influence whether Roth contributions or conversions make sense.

Phase 1: Final Working Years

During your final working years, you still have earned income and are likely in one of your highest lifetime brackets. In this phase, Roth contributions may make sense if you expect even higher future tax rates, but Traditional contributions may be appropriate if retirement income will drop substantially. Strategic Roth conversions can also make sense up to the top of your current bracket—and occasionally beyond—if long-term modeling supports it.

Importantly, IRMAA is not yet a concern until age 63 due to the two-year Medicare lookback, and Social Security taxation is not yet in play. This makes the late fifties and early sixties a relatively clean environment for bracket management.

Phase 2: Retirement to Age 62

Once earned income stops, many couples experience a temporary drop in taxable income. This period—before Social Security begins—can create one of the most attractive Roth conversion windows of your lifetime. You may be able to fill lower tax brackets intentionally while controlling how much income appears on your return.

Because Social Security has not yet been claimed, you do not have to worry about increasing its taxation. For couples retiring before 62, this phase can be a powerful opportunity to reduce future RMD exposure.

Phase 3: Age 62–70 (Social Security Decision Window)

Between age 62 and 70, you have flexibility in when to claim Social Security. Claiming early provides income but may increase the taxable portion of benefits if you are also doing conversions. Delaying benefits increases future guaranteed income but may provide more room for conversions in the present.

This is not just a Social Security decision; it is a tax coordination decision. The interaction between conversion income and Social Security taxation is complex, and we will examine that in greater detail in Chapter 6.

Phase 4: Retirement to Age 65 (Premium Tax Credit Window)

If you retire before age 65 and are not yet on Medicare, you may be purchasing private insurance through the exchange. In this window, your income directly impacts eligibility for the Premium Tax Credit (PTC). Roth conversions that increase AGI can reduce or eliminate those credits, effectively creating a hidden marginal tax rate.

For early retirees, this healthcare subsidy often becomes the dominant tax consideration. We will cover the PTC mechanics in Chapter 6, but it must be modeled carefully when considering conversions before Medicare.

Phase 5: Age 63–65 (IRMAA Lookback Begins)

IRMAA premiums are based on your MAGI from two years prior. That means income at age 63 affects Medicare premiums at age 65. As a result, Roth conversions in your early sixties can increase Medicare costs later if they push you over IRMAA thresholds.

This is where bracket management becomes more delicate. You may still convert—but you must weigh whether temporarily crossing an IRMAA threshold is worth the long-term tax benefit.

Phase 6: Age 65–70 (Medicare in Effect)

After age 65, the Premium Tax Credit is no longer an issue, but IRMAA is still in effect. This period marks the final stretch during which Social Security may still be delayed, and RMDs have not yet begun. For many couples, this is one of the remaining strategic conversion windows.

You may intentionally convert up to—but not through—an IRMAA threshold. Alternatively, you may decide to exceed a threshold for a short period to reduce future RMDs and lower premiums for the next decade.

Phase 7: Age 70–73/75 (Final Pre-RMD Window)

By age 70, Social Security has typically been claimed, and Qualified Charitable Distributions become available at age 70½. This is the final clean stretch before RMDs begin at age 73 (or 75 for younger cohorts). Income stacking becomes more complex, but strategic conversions can still meaningfully reduce the size of future mandatory distributions.

This window is often underutilized. Many retirees assume they are "done" with Roth planning once Medicare begins, when in reality this may be the last meaningful opportunity to reshape the tax trajectory of the next twenty years.

Phase 8: RMD Age and Beyond

Once RMDs begin, your flexibility narrows but does not disappear. You must take the RMD first, but you can still convert additional amounts above it. In some cases, it may make sense to temporarily fill up an IRMAA bracket for a few years to reduce future RMDs and fall back under a threshold for a decade or more.

Conversions during RMD years may also be motivated by legacy planning. Moving money from Traditional accounts to

Roth can reduce the tax burden on heirs and create more predictable after-tax inheritance outcomes.

The common theme across all phases is this: Roth strategy is dynamic. The right answer at age 60 may not be the right answer at age 67, 72, or 78. Effective planning requires ongoing modeling, not a one-time decision.

Conclusion: Clarity Without Fatigue

If this chapter feels dense, that is because it is. Roth strategy touches tax brackets, Medicare premiums, Social Security taxation, healthcare subsidies, legacy planning, and Required Minimum Distributions. It is one of the few decisions in retirement planning that meaningfully affects every other area of your financial life.

But complexity does not mean paralysis.

In Chapter 1, we discussed **Financial Fatigue**—the mental exhaustion that sets in when decisions feel overwhelming and interconnected. Roth planning can trigger that fatigue quickly because every lever affects three others. When that happens, the temptation is to simplify the decision into a slogan: "Always do Roth," or "Always defer taxes." Both are wrong.

The better response is not avoidance. It is modeling.

You need a plan for each phase of your life, and you need it this year. It starts with understanding which phase you are in now, what thresholds are active, and what your likely future trajectory looks like. If you are feeling overwhelmed, skip ahead to Chapter 10, where we discuss how to implement this with the right tools—or the right professional help.

In the meantime, remember the central principle of this chapter:

Pay taxes at the lowest rate you can across your lifetime—not only now or only later.

In the next chapter, we will shift from retirement accounts to **brokerage strategies**. Because even if you optimize Roth and Traditional accounts perfectly, how you manage taxable investments can either reinforce—or undo—your tax strategy.

Chapter Summary

- Traditional accounts defer taxes; Roth accounts prepay them.
- Contributions are limited and require earned income; conversions are unlimited but fully taxable.
- The Roth decision is a tax-rate arbitrage: pay now or later at the lowest lifetime rate.
- Small percentage differences in tax rates compound into large lifetime dollar differences.
- Advanced thresholds such as IRMAA, NIIT, Social Security taxation, and deduction phase-outs materially affect your true marginal rate.
- Required Minimum Distributions can push retirees into higher brackets and additional thresholds if not planned for early.
- Roth strategy changes across life phases and must be revisited regularly.

Brokerage Strategies

Action Items

1. Identify your current marginal effective tax rate (including federal, state, and any threshold stacking).
2. Estimate your likely retirement income sources: pensions, Social Security, RMDs, and brokerage income.
3. Determine which Roth phase you are currently in and whether conversions make sense this year.
4. If you do not already have a Roth IRA open, open one and fund it with at least **$100** to start your 5-year clock. If you do not already use Charles Schwab, Fidelity, or Vanguard, consider opening an account at **Charles Schwab**.
5. If you are unsure how your RMDs, IRMAA, and Social Security interact, model it—or work with someone who can.

No action: no credit. The goal is not to understand the Roth strategy. The goal is to use it.

Chapter 5

Tax-Effective Ways to Grow Non-Retirement Accounts

Don't skip this chapter until you've finished the "Can I Skip This Chapter?" section. Even if you don't have a brokerage account, at least read through that section.

In Chapter 4, we focused on retirement accounts—Traditional and Roth. In this chapter, we turn to the money outside those accounts. For many couples over fifty, brokerage accounts offer flexibility, options, and opportunities. They also represent hidden tax drag if unmanaged.

This chapter matters because the tax code treats "owners" and "loaners" very differently. The way you choose to make money inside your brokerage account has a direct impact on how much you keep after taxes. And as we established in Chapter 1, the goal is not to minimize taxes in isolation, but to maximize after-tax wealth over your lifetime.

Two Ways to Make Money

In *3D Retirement Income*, I introduced the concept of being an **Owner** or a **Loaner**.

You can loan your money to businesses and governments and earn interest. Or you can own businesses and participate in their growth and profits. Both have a place in a portfolio. But they are not taxed the same way.

Inside retirement accounts, the tax difference is muted because growth is tax-deferred. Inside brokerage accounts, the tax difference becomes far more significant.

Loaners

Loaners buy interest-bearing investments. This includes bonds, bond funds, CDs, Treasuries, and money market funds. When you loan money, you receive interest in return.

Interest income is taxed as ordinary income. It does not receive preferential capital gains treatment. If you are in the 22% bracket, you generally pay 22% on that interest, plus potential state taxes and possibly NIIT.

There is no special rate. No stacking advantage. No 0% bracket for interest income.

Being a loaner provides stability and predictability. But from a tax perspective inside a brokerage account, it is the least efficient way to earn returns.

Owners

Owners buy businesses. When you own a mutual fund or ETF that holds publicly traded companies, you are a partial owner of thousands of businesses.

Owners make money in two ways:

- Growth in business value (capital appreciation)
- Profits paid to owners (dividends)

Capital appreciation is generally taxed only when realized. Qualified dividends and long-term capital gains are subject to preferential tax treatment. This makes ownership structurally more tax-efficient than lending inside brokerage accounts.

In most long-term scenarios, being an owner has historically produced higher total returns than being a loaner. When you combine higher return potential with preferential tax treatment, ownership becomes even more compelling inside taxable accounts.

In 3D Retirement Income, I advocate for higher ownership than most conventional strategies, but in a way that makes strategic sense. You can get 3D Retirement Income from Amazon and Audible, or for free at RetireMentorship.com.

Can I Skip This Chapter?

You can skip this chapter if *both* of these are true:

1. You don't have any brokerage accounts.
2. The total non-retirement money you have is less than a year's worth of expenses.

Why the second stipulation? Some of you have non-retirement money in CDs, savings accounts, or annuities that should probably be invested differently. If you have less than a year's worth of expenses in bank products, that's likely fine. But if you have hundreds of thousands sitting in low-yield accounts because you're unsure what to do with them, you should understand how brokerage accounts work.

If nearly all your assets are in Traditional and Roth accounts, and you have very little outside of checking and savings, you can safely skip this chapter and conserve your mental energy. You still get credit for reading the book.

What Are Brokerage Accounts?

Before diving into strategy, we need to clarify terminology.

"Non-qualified" is a tax classification. It simply means the account does not receive special retirement tax treatment under IRS rules. It is not a judgment about quality. It distinguishes these accounts from qualified retirement accounts like 401(k)s and IRAs.

A "brokerage account" is the container. It allows you to hold multiple investment types in one place, including stocks, bonds, ETFs, mutual funds, CDs, and Treasuries. The brokerage is the platform. The tax classification determines how the IRS treats activities that occur inside it.

In this chapter, I will primarily use the term "brokerage account" because it is clearer and more practical.

How Brokerage Accounts Are Taxed

Brokerage accounts are taxed along the way. Unlike Traditional and Roth accounts, there is no shelter from annual taxation.

Capital Gains vs. Ordinary Income

The tax code distinguishes between ordinary income and capital gains. Ordinary income includes wages, IRA distributions, interest, and non-qualified dividends. Capital gains result from selling an investment for more than its cost basis.

Ordinary income is taxed at your marginal tax bracket. Capital gains may receive preferential treatment, depending on how long you held the investment and your total taxable income.

Understanding this difference is critical when deciding what to hold inside a brokerage account.

Long-Term Capital Gains and Qualified Dividends

If you hold an investment for more than one year before selling, any gain is considered long-term. Long-term capital gains are taxed at 0%, 15%, or 20%, depending on your taxable income.

Qualified dividends receive the same preferential treatment. These rates are generally lower than ordinary income rates. For many retirees, portions of long-term gains can even be taxed at 0%.

So what makes a dividend "qualified"? In general, the dividend must be paid by a U.S. corporation (or certain qualified foreign corporations), and you must have held the stock or fund for a required minimum holding period—typically more than 60 days during the 121-day period surrounding the ex-dividend date (the cutoff date set by the company that determines who is entitled to receive the upcoming dividend—if you buy the stock on or after the ex-dividend date, you will not receive that dividend). If those conditions are not met, the dividend is treated as ordinary.

Broad-market U.S. equity index funds and ETFs tend to produce a high percentage of qualified dividends because they hold large, established corporations that meet the IRS requirements. Actively traded funds, certain international funds, REIT funds, bond funds, and high-yield income funds often generate more ordinary (non-qualified) dividends. REIT distributions in particular are generally taxed as ordinary income, even though they may appear on your 1099-DIV alongside qualified dividends.

Understanding what type of fund you own—and how its distributions are classified—can materially impact your after-tax return. This preferential structure is one reason ownership can be more tax-efficient than lending inside brokerage accounts.

Short-Term Capital Gains, Ordinary Dividends, and Interest

Short-term capital gains—investments sold within and including one year—are taxed as ordinary income. Ordinary dividends are also taxed at ordinary income rates. Interest income from bonds, CDs, savings accounts, and money market funds is fully taxed at ordinary income rates.

These types of income are often paid regularly. Interest may be paid monthly or quarterly. Bond funds and money market funds typically distribute income monthly. Many mutual funds and ETFs pay dividends quarterly, though some pay annually. Whether you reinvest those payments or have them sent to your bank account does not change the tax treatment. Reinvested income is still taxable in the year it is paid.

These amounts are reported to you on Form 1099-INT (for interest) and Form 1099-DIV (for dividends and capital gain distributions). Ordinary dividends appear in Box 1a of the 1099-DIV, while qualified dividends are listed separately in Box 1b. These totals flow to Schedule B of your tax return if they exceed certain thresholds and ultimately appear on your Form 1040 as part of your total income.

Unlike wages and many retirement distributions, taxes are generally not withheld from interest and dividend payments. As a result, significant brokerage income can surprise investors at tax time. It is not uncommon for retirees with growing taxable accounts to owe money in April simply because no taxes were withheld throughout the year.

There is no preferential bracket for these categories. This is why high-turnover funds, high-yield bond funds, and heavily traded strategies can create unnecessary tax drag inside brokerage accounts.

Income Stacking

Capital gains do not exist in a separate tax universe. On your tax return, everything is first combined.

On the 2025 Form 1040, both your ordinary income and your capital gains flow into "Taxable Income" on Line 15. At that point, they are lumped into a single number. However, when the IRS calculates your actual tax on Line 16, it does not simply multiply that total by your marginal bracket. Instead, it uses a separate worksheet (or the Qualified Dividends and Capital Gain Tax Worksheet) to effectively split the income back apart and apply different rates to different layers.

Here is what that means in practice: ordinary income fills up the lower brackets first. Long-term capital gains and qualified dividends then stack on top of that ordinary income and are taxed at 0%, 15%, or 20%, depending on where the total taxable income lands. The 1040 shows a single taxable income amount, but the tax calculation treats portions of it differently.

Consider Steve & Rachel. With roughly $450,000 of gross income during their peak earning years and substantial retirement contributions, their taxable income still places them well above the 0% capital gains threshold. Any additional long-term gains or qualified dividends they realize will almost certainly be taxed at 15%. Because their Modified Adjusted Gross Income also exceeds $250,000, those gains are generally subject to the 3.8% Net Investment Income Tax as well. For them, every additional dollar of long-term gain is likely taxed at 18.8% federally, before state taxes.

Now contrast that with Bob & Sue. They have $50,000 of Social Security and $50,000 of pension income. Depending on how much of their Social Security is taxable and how they manage other withdrawals in a given year, their taxable income could fall within or even below the 0% long-term capital gains bracket. If they intentionally limit additional IRA distributions in a particular year, they may be able to realize brokerage gains and pay 0% federal tax on those gains.

This is the power of stacking. The same $40,000 of capital gains could cost Steve & Rachel over $7,000 in federal taxes, while costing Bob & Sue nothing in a carefully planned year. In later sections on tax gain harvesting and tax loss harvesting, we will walk through how to intentionally use this stacking effect rather than accidentally triggering it.

Net Investment Income Tax

The Net Investment Income Tax (NIIT) adds 3.8% to investment income once Modified Adjusted Gross Income exceeds $250,000 for Married Filing Jointly. It applies to interest, dividends, capital gains, rental income, and certain business income.

Crossing this threshold can increase a 15% capital gains rate to 18.8%. Managing realization timing and total income can help you avoid triggering this additional layer unnecessarily.

Brokerage Strategies

Before jumping into specific tactics, we need to anchor the priorities correctly.

After-tax wealth matters more than total return. Total return matters more than whether returns come from dividends or appreciation. Dividends versus growth is not a moral decision; it is a tax and planning decision.

The goal is to keep more of what your portfolio earns, not simply to generate income.

Asset Location

Asset location asks a simple question: which investments belong in which accounts?

It is not enough to decide your allocation between stocks and bonds. You must also decide where those stocks and bonds live.

Tax-inefficient assets are generally better inside tax-deferred accounts. These include:

- High-yield bonds
- REITs
- Actively managed, high-turnover funds

Why? Because the income they generate is taxed at ordinary income rates. High-yield bonds distribute large amounts of interest each year. REITs distribute income that is typically taxed as ordinary income. High-turnover funds regularly realize short-term capital gains that are also taxed as ordinary income. If those assets are in a brokerage account, you are paying taxes on that income every single year.

Inside a Traditional IRA or 401(k), however, that income grows tax-deferred. You do not receive a 1099 each year. You defer the tax until distribution, when you may be in a lower bracket.

Tax-efficient assets are often better suited for brokerage accounts. These include:

- Broad-market index ETFs
- Low-turnover mutual funds
- Individual stocks held long-term

These investments tend to generate fewer short-term gains and a higher percentage of qualified dividends. Much of their return comes from unrealized appreciation, which you control.

If you enjoy trading stocks, dabbling in active strategies, or making short-term bets, do that inside a qualified retirement account. Frequent trading in a brokerage account creates short-term capital gains, and the IRS becomes your silent business partner. In a Roth IRA or a Traditional IRA, you can trade without creating an annual tax bill.

Small changes in asset location can improve after-tax returns without altering your risk profile.

Tax Loss Harvesting

Tax loss harvesting is not about "taking losses." It is about preserving after-tax wealth during downturns.

Imagine Steve & Rachel experience a significant market decline in their brokerage account. A fund they purchased for $200,000 is now worth $140,000. They could sell that fund, realize a $60,000 capital loss, and immediately purchase a similar—but not substantially identical—fund that is also down in value. They remain invested in the market and participate in the recovery.

That $60,000 loss first offsets any capital gains realized during the year. If they have no gains, they can deduct up to $3,000 per year against ordinary income. In their high bracket, that $3,000 deduction could save them 32% federally—nearly $1,000 per year—plus state taxes. The remaining loss carries forward indefinitely.

Eventually, the replacement investment will recover. When they sell it at a gain in the future, they will owe capital gains tax. But here is the key: they deducted the loss at 32% (plus potential state taxes) and may eventually pay 15% or 18.8% (15% + NIIT) on the gain. That is a favorable rate arbitrage.

Two cautions are important.

First, you must avoid the wash sale rule. Selling a fund and repurchasing the same or substantially identical fund within 30 days disallows the loss.

Second, realized gains in the future will first absorb carryforward capital losses before any $3,000 ordinary deduction is applied. If you harvest a large loss and then immediately realize gains in the same year, the benefit may simply offset those gains rather than reduce ordinary income.

Harvesting works best when done systematically and strategically—not reactively.

Tax Gain Harvesting

Tax gain harvesting is the mirror image of loss harvesting.

Bob & Sue may find themselves in years where their taxable income is low enough to qualify for the 0% long-term capital gains bracket. If they have appreciated brokerage assets, they can intentionally sell shares, realize gains at 0%, and immediately repurchase the same or similar investments to reset their cost basis higher.

This strategy reduces embedded gains for the future. When they later need to sell for spending—or when the surviving spouse files as single—they will have less taxable gain per dollar sold.

Careful tax-lot management is critical. Rather than selling entire positions, they can select specific high-basis lots to control the amount of gain realized. Most custodians allow specific lot identification, which provides far more precision than default FIFO (first-in, first-out) accounting.

In the transition years to retirement—before large RMDs begin—this strategy can gradually cleanse a brokerage account of low-basis positions without paying federal tax.

Appreciation vs. Income

Total return is what ultimately grows wealth. But how that return is delivered matters for taxes.

For high-income accumulators like Steve & Rachel, shifting brokerage assets toward growth-oriented investments can reduce annual tax drag. A fund that earns 8% total return but distributes only 1% in dividends leaves 7% as unrealized appreciation. That 7% is not taxed until realized.

Compare that to a high-dividend strategy that earns 8% total return but distributes 5% annually. That 5% is taxed every year, whether reinvested or not. Over time, that ongoing tax friction compounds.

If Steve & Rachel harvest losses during a downturn, they could amplify the benefit by reinvesting into more growth-focused funds, reducing future dividend taxation while preserving long-term return potential.

Bob & Sue may face the opposite decision. If they desire supplemental income regardless of market fluctuations, higher-dividend investments can provide steady cash flow. If their total taxable income is low enough, those qualified dividends may fall into the 0% capital gains bracket.

However, even Bob & Sue must be careful. Large dividend distributions increase Adjusted Gross Income and can affect the taxation of Social Security benefits. In some years, they may prefer growth-oriented funds to control when gains are realized and better manage provisional income. We will explore that interaction in Chapter 6.

The right mix is not static. It evolves as your income, spending needs, and tax brackets change.

Managing NIIT

For high-income earners like Steve & Rachel, the Net Investment Income Tax is often unavoidable during peak earning years. Any additional long-term gains or qualified dividends are likely taxed at 15% plus 3.8% NIIT.

However, timing still matters.

If they are considering selling a highly appreciated position, they should evaluate whether doing so now at 18.8% makes sense or whether deferring until retirement, when their income may fall below the $250,000 MAGI threshold, is preferable. Avoiding NIIT alone reduces the federal rate from 18.8% to 15%.

Similarly, spreading large sales over multiple years can prevent excessive gains from being stacked into a single tax year and pushing more income into higher brackets.

NIIT management is not about avoiding success. It is about choosing when that success becomes taxable.

Maximizing the Step-Up in Basis

Brokerage accounts receive a step-up in basis at death. Appreciated investments are reset to fair market value, eliminating embedded capital gains for heirs.

For Bob & Sue, this has powerful implications. If they hold appreciated assets jointly, the surviving spouse may receive a full or partial step-up in basis depending on state law and account structure. In community property states, the entire account may step up in value. In common law states, generally, only the deceased spouse's half of the estate receives a step-up.

Holding assets in joint tenancy rather than in an individual name can affect how the basis is adjusted at the first death. Coordinating titling with estate planning documents is essential.

Eventually, when assets pass to children, the step-up eliminates capital gains tax on lifetime appreciation. This is a significant advantage over Traditional retirement accounts, which pass with embedded ordinary income tax liability, and over non-qualified annuities discussed in Chapter 3, which do not receive a step-up in basis.

From a legacy perspective, it can make sense to spend down pre-tax retirement accounts first and preserve brokerage assets when appropriate. That decision must be coordinated with lifetime tax brackets, RMDs, and charitable goals.

The step-up in basis is one of the most powerful, yet underappreciated, tax features available to long-term investors.

Chapter Summary

- You can make money as an owner or a loaner, and they are taxed differently.
- Interest, short-term gains, and ordinary dividends are taxed at ordinary income rates.
- Long-term capital gains and qualified dividends are treated preferentially, but only after they are added on top of ordinary income.
- Your 1040 combines income on Line 15, but the IRS applies different rates behind the scenes to calculate Line 16 tax.
- NIIT can add 3.8% to investment income at higher MAGI levels, increasing your effective capital gains rate.
- Asset location can materially reduce annual tax drag without changing your overall allocation.
- Tax loss harvesting allows you to deduct losses at high ordinary rates and potentially pay lower capital gains rates later.
- Tax gain harvesting allows you to intentionally use the 0% capital gains bracket to reset basis.
- Appreciation provides more tax control than forced income, but income-focused strategies can be appropriate in certain retirement phases.
- Brokerage accounts receive a step-up in basis at death, making them powerful tools for legacy planning.

Taken together, brokerage strategy is not about chasing dividends or avoiding taxes at all costs. It is about coordinating investments, timing, and tax brackets to maximize after-tax wealth over your lifetime and for the next generation.

Social Security & Medical Tax Planning

Action Items

1. Identify whether your brokerage assets are primarily owner assets or loaner assets, and determine whether that aligns with your tax bracket and phase of life.
2. Review your most recent 1099-INT and 1099-DIV. Highlight interest, ordinary dividends, qualified dividends, and capital gain distributions.
3. Compare your dividend yield to your total return. Ask whether too much of your return is being forced into taxable income each year.
4. Evaluate whether tax-inefficient assets (high-yield bonds, REITs, high-turnover funds) could be relocated into retirement accounts.
5. Review unrealized gains and losses and determine whether a tax loss or tax gain harvesting strategy makes sense this year.
6. Check your Modified Adjusted Gross Income and determine whether additional gains would trigger or avoid NIIT.

7. If legacy planning is important to you, review how your brokerage accounts are titled and whether they are positioned to maximize step-up in basis.

Brokerage strategy rewards intentionality. Small, consistent adjustments—made year after year—can compound into significant lifetime tax savings

Chapter 6

Optimizing Taxes in Retirement

Social Security and healthcare are two of the most significant financial forces in retirement. One provides income. The other consumes it. And both are deeply intertwined with the tax code.

For many couples over fifty, Social Security will represent a substantial portion of retirement income. It is also one of the few income sources where the amount you receive, the timing of your receipt, and how it is taxed are all within your control. That makes it powerful—and potentially dangerous if misunderstood.

Healthcare, meanwhile, is often the largest unpredictable expense retirees face. The way you insure against medical costs—before and after Medicare—directly impacts your tax return. Income levels determine premium credits, Medicare surcharges, and hidden marginal rates that don't show up neatly on a 1040.

In this chapter, we'll break this into three major sections:

- Social Security Tax Planning
- Pre-Retirement Medical Planning
- Medicare & IRMAA Tax Planning

By the end, you'll understand how these systems interact with your retirement income plan—and how to avoid accidentally increasing your largest lifetime expense.

Social Security Tax Planning

How Social Security Works

Social Security is earned through work credits. In simple terms, you pay into the system through payroll taxes (12.4% Social Security tax on earned income, split between employee and employer), and your benefit is calculated based on your highest 35 years of earnings, adjusted for inflation.

Your benefit is determined in three steps. First, the Social Security Administration indexes your earnings for inflation and calculates your Average Indexed Monthly Earnings (AIME). Second, AIME is used in a progressive formula that replaces a higher percentage of lower earnings and a lower percentage of higher earnings. The result is your Primary Insurance Amount (PIA). Finally, your claiming age permanently adjusts that PIA up or down.

You can claim benefits as early as age 62. Your Full Retirement Age (FRA) is between 66 and 67, depending on your birth year. If you claim before your FRA, your benefit is permanently reduced. If you delay beyond FRA, your benefit increases by roughly 8% per year until age 70.

Here's the basic structure:

- Claim at 62 → Permanent reduction (up to ~30% lower than FRA).
- Claim at FRA → 100% of your Primary Insurance Amount (PIA).
- Delay to 70 → Roughly 24–32% higher than the FRA benefit.

Spousal benefits allow one spouse to receive up to 50% of the other's FRA benefit if higher. Survivor benefits allow the surviving spouse to step into the larger of the two benefits after the first death.

This matters greatly for Chuck & Diane. Chuck likely has the higher benefit based on earnings history. If he delays until 70 and Diane survives him, she may receive his larger benefit for the rest of her life. Longevity planning and tax planning intersect here.

Social Security is not just an income decision. It is a longevity hedge, a survivor planning tool, and a tax variable.

How Social Security Is Taxed

Social Security can be:

- 0% taxable
- Up to 50% taxable
- Up to 85% taxable

The keywords are "up to." The maximum that can be included in taxable income is 85% of your benefit. It is never 100%.

The taxation is based on something called **Provisional Income**, calculated as:

Adjusted Gross Income

- Tax-exempt municipal bond interest
- 50% of Social Security benefits

For Married Filing Jointly:

- Below $32,000 → 0% taxable
- $32,000–$44,000 → Up to 50% taxable
- Above $44,000 → Up to 85% taxable

Those thresholds—$32,000 and $44,000—have not changed since 1984 and 1993, respectively. They are not indexed for inflation. That means more retirees drift into higher taxation every year simply because nominal income rises. Congress effectively created a slow-motion tax increase that compounds over time.

But crossing $44,000 does not automatically mean that 85% of your Social Security benefits become taxable. The formula is layered.

Let's calculate Bob & Sue's see taxable amount using the official method. The method for calculating it is somewhat complex. Your tax return does it automatically. So does the calculator in the Book Bonus. Using that is much simpler.

Bob & Sue receive:

- $50,000 Social Security
- $50,000 pension income

Provisional Income:

- $50,000 pension
- $25,000 (half of SS)
- = $75,000 provisional income

Taxable Social Security:

- Run the calculation online:
- = $32,350 is taxed

Bob & Sue are over the $44,000, but they do not have 85% of their Social Security taxed. They have $32,350 of their $50,000 taxed. That equals 64.7% of their benefit.

This is an important distinction. Many retirees assume that once they cross $44,000, they are "fully taxed." In reality, the formula phases in gradually.

However, additional income will push that taxable portion higher until it caps at 85%.

Now, suppose Bob & Sue take an additional $20,000 in IRA withdrawals.

- New provisional income: $95,000
- Formula for Taxation: $49,350
- Find 85% cap: 85% of $50,000 = $42,500
- Take the lower amount: $42,500

Since $42,500 is lower, they hit the maximum. An additional $20,000 withdrawal caused an additional $10,150 of Social Security to become taxable. This is where the effective marginal rate begins to matter.

Social Security Interaction

Because provisional income includes AGI plus half of Social Security, other income sources directly affect how much of your Social Security becomes taxable.

Examples of income that increase provisional income:

- IRA withdrawals
- 401(k) distributions
- Roth conversions
- Capital gains
- Dividends
- Rental income
- Municipal bond interest

Yes—even tax-free municipal bond interest counts in provisional income.

This means harvesting a capital gain in a brokerage account (Chapter 5) or executing a Roth conversion (Chapter 4) may cause more of your Social Security to become taxable.

Before executing either strategy, you should ask:

"If I add $10,000 of income, how much additional Social Security becomes taxable?"

If $8,500 of Social Security shifts from tax-free to taxable, your "$10,000 Roth conversion" may functionally add $18,500 to taxable income.

Tax planning must be integrated. Strategies in isolation can create hidden consequences.

Effective Marginal Tax Rates

Let's define three critical terms:

Marginal Tax Rate – The rate you pay on your next dollar of taxable income.

Effective Tax Rate – Your total tax divided by gross income.

Effective Marginal Rate – The true cost of your next dollar when accounting for additional triggered taxes.

Using Bob & Sue's earlier example, suppose they are in the 12% federal bracket.

If they withdraw $10,000 more from their IRA, and $8,500 of Social Security becomes taxable, then $18,500 is taxed at 12%.

$18,500 × 12% = $2,220 tax.

$2,220 ÷ $10,000 = 22.2% effective marginal rate.

They thought they were in the 12% bracket. They were effectively paying over 22%.

If that additional income also triggered IRMAA two years later, the effective rate climbs even higher.

This stacking effect of the effective margin tax rate is why Social Security planning cannot be separated from Roth planning.

Social Security Timing Decisions

There are four major decision factors:

1. Longevity

Many people evaluate Social Security in a vacuum using break-even analysis. "If I live past age 83, delaying wins."

But longevity planning must consider:

- Spousal life expectancy
- Survivor income needs
- Inflation protection
- Tax impacts

Delaying increases guaranteed, inflation-adjusted income for life.

2. Income Sequencing

If you delay Social Security, you will have to draw from other sources.

For Chuck & Diane, delaying may require larger IRA withdrawals early. That could reduce future RMDs but increase current taxes. However, those early withdrawals may occur in lower brackets before RMDs begin.

Claiming early preserves investment accounts but reduces guaranteed income.

3. Taxation

If Chuck & Diane delay Social Security until 70, their early retirement years (62–70) may present low-income windows ideal for Roth conversions.

Alternatively, claiming earlier increases the Social Security portion of total income, potentially reducing IRA withdrawals needed and altering provisional income dynamics.

The Social Security decision should be modeled alongside the Roth strategy, not separately.

4. Legacy

Social Security income dies with you (except survivor benefits). IRA and brokerage accounts pass to heirs.

Some couples intentionally claim Social Security earlier to preserve investable assets for a legacy. Others delay to reduce longevity risk and maximize lifetime guaranteed income. The decision is multidimensional—not emotional.

Social Security is not just a government benefit. It is a tax lever. Before claiming, harvesting gains, or converting to Roth, run projections that include:

- Provisional income
- Effective Marginal Rate
- IRMAA thresholds

- RMD projections

Software matters here. A spreadsheet guess is not sufficient.

Pre-Retirement Medical Tax Planning

Working Health Insurance & HSAs

If you are still working and enrolled in a High Deductible Health Plan (HDHP), you have access to one of the most powerful accounts in the tax code: the Health Savings Account.

HSAs are triple tax advantaged:

- Contributions reduce taxable income (above-the-line deduction).
- Growth is tax-deferred.
- Withdrawals for qualified medical expenses are tax-free.

For 2026, HSA contribution limits are projected to be approximately:

- Individual coverage: ~$4,300
- Family coverage: ~$8,600
- Catch-up (age 55+): +$1,000 per spouse

Unlike FSAs, HSAs are not "use it or lose it." The account is yours permanently. It can be invested, rolled over, and used decades later.

The strategy many miss is this: pay current medical expenses out of pocket and allow the HSA to grow invested. You can reimburse yourself for qualified expenses years later, provided you kept receipts.

If invested for 15–20 years, it can compound tax-free and be used for:

- Medicare Part B premiums
- Medicare Part D premiums
- Out-of-pocket medical costs
- Long-term care expenses (within limits)

Healthcare is a future certainty. The HSA lets you pre-fund it tax efficiently.

Retiring Before Medicare (Marketplace Planning)

If you retire before age 65, you will use the Health Insurance Marketplace. Premiums are based on income, specifically Modified Adjusted Gross Income (MAGI).

The Premium Tax Credit phases in and out based on income relative to the Federal Poverty Level (FPL). Even small income increases can materially reduce subsidies.

This creates a powerful planning window between retirement and Medicare.

Strategies to control income from retirement to age 65:

- Draw from brokerage accounts with high basis (minimal gains).
- Harvest gains strategically to stay within subsidy ranges.
- Delay Social Security to suppress provisional income.
- Spread Roth conversions carefully within subsidy thresholds.

For Chuck & Diane, retiring at 62 may mean intentionally keeping MAGI low for three years to qualify for substantial premium subsidies, potentially saving tens of thousands of dollars before Medicare begins.

Medical insurance planning in early retirement is income planning.

Medicare Tax Planning

How Medicare Works

Medicare begins at age 65.
It has four major parts:

- Part A: Hospital insurance (generally premium-free if work credits met).
- Part B: Outpatient and physician services (monthly premium).
- Part D: Prescription drug coverage (monthly premium).
- Part C (Advantage): Bundled private alternative to Parts A & B (often includes D).

Most retirees choose between Original Medicare (A & B) with a Medigap supplement or a Medicare Advantage plan.

Part B and Part D premiums are income-sensitive.

That sensitivity is called IRMAA.

Income Related Medicare Adjustment Amount (IRMAA)

IRMAA increases Medicare Part B and D premiums based on MAGI from two years prior.

It does not appear on your tax return. It simply increases your monthly premium. Many retirees are surprised when they receive a letter from Social Security informing them their premiums are increasing because of their income two years ago.

IRMAA is threshold-based—not progressive. Crossing $1 over a threshold triggers the full higher premium for the entire year.

2026 IRMAA Thresholds (Married Filing Jointly)

MAGI (2-Year Lookback)	Part B Monthly Premium (Per Person)	Part D Surcharge (Per Person)
≤ $218,000	$203	$0
$218,001–$274,000	+ $81	+ $15
$274,001–$342,000	+ $203	+ $38
$342,001–$410,000	+ $325	+ $60
$410,001–$750,000	+ $446	+ $83
> $750,000	+ $487	+ $91

If both spouses are on Medicare, crossing the first IRMAA threshold could increase premiums by roughly $96 per person per month (Part B + D combined), or over $2,300 per year for the household.

And remember: this increase lasts for the entire year.

Key notes:

- IRMAA is based on MAGI, not taxable income.
- Roth conversions increase MAGI.
- Capital gains increase MAGI.

- Municipal bond interest increases MAGI.
- Social Security taxation does not directly determine IRMAA.

This is separate from provisional income.

Three income definitions. Three consequences.

Medicare Tax Planning

If you are not yet on Medicare:

You may consider larger Roth conversions before age 63, because IRMAA begins affecting premiums at age 65 with a two-year lookback.

Example:

Convert heavily at age 61–62 → No IRMAA impact.

Convert heavily at 63 → Impacts premiums at 65.

Timing matters.

If you are already on Medicare:

Be aware of IRMAA thresholds.

If you are going to get close to a threshold, it may make sense to:

- Convert only up to just under the threshold.
- Or if you cross over the threshold, convert additional funds to fill up the current tax bracket.

For example, if Chuck & Diane are $5,000 over an IRMAA threshold due to a Roth conversion, they may pay an additional $2,000 in Medicare premiums. That effectively adds 40% to that $5,000 decision.

This is why marginal effective rates must include IRMAA.

Model it.

Conclusion

Social Security and healthcare are not passive systems. They are dynamic tax levers.

- Social Security interacts with provisional income.
- Roth conversions alter Social Security taxation and IRMAA.
- Capital gains affect MAGI and Medicare premiums.
- Marketplace subsidies reward income control before age 65.

All three systems stack.

If you ignore them, you may unknowingly pay thousands more per year.

If you coordinate them, you can flatten lifetime tax brackets and preserve more after-tax wealth.

This chapter is not about minimizing this year's taxes.

It is about optimizing decades.

Chapter Summary
- Social Security taxation phases in gradually and caps at 85%.
- The $32,000 and $44,000 thresholds are not indexed for inflation.
- Provisional income includes municipal bond interest and 50% of Social Security.
- Effective marginal tax rates can exceed stated brackets due to stacking.
- Timing Social Security affects longevity, taxation, income sequencing, and legacy.
- HSAs offer triple tax advantages when invested properly.
- Early retirees can manage Marketplace subsidies by controlling MAGI.
- Medicare premiums increase via IRMAA based on MAGI from two years prior.
- IRMAA is threshold-based, not progressive.
- Roth conversion timing relative to Medicare age matters significantly.

Action Items
1. Calculate your exact Social Security taxable amount using the official worksheet.
2. Before doing a Roth conversion, evaluate its impact on Social Security taxation and IRMAA.
3. If retiring before 65, project Marketplace premiums under different MAGI levels.
4. Identify your IRMAA thresholds and monitor them annually once on Medicare.
5. If still working with an HDHP, evaluate maximizing your HSA and investing it.
6. Run a coordinated retirement income projection that integrates Social Security, RMDs, Roth conversions, capital gains, and Medicare premiums.

Charitable Giving Strategies

Chapter 7

Skip the IRS and Give More

Jesus said, "Give to Caesar what is Caesar's, and to God what is God's." The statement perfectly encapsulates the principles of charitable giving strategies. We'll pay the taxes we owe; we don't want to pay extra. And if we can pay less to Caesar and more to churches and charities, even better.

We do not give so that we can get a tax break. We give so that we can experience the joy of generosity, support the causes we care about, and help those in need. *And* if we can *also* secure a tax break, we should take advantage of it.

Paying less in taxes due to charitable giving strategies means we can realize one of three benefits.

1. We can give the *same* amount with *less* impact on our budget and assets.
2. We can give *more* with the *same* impact on our budget and assets.
3. We can split the difference (give slightly *more* while having slightly *less* impact).

With these potential benefits, why wouldn't we want to know some of the best strategies available? Beyond that, **I believe we have a moral obligation to divert tax payments to charity.**

Who is going to do a better job with our money? The government (with its deficit budget, ballooning spending, and wasteful allocation of funds), or the charities of your choice (who are on the ground in the communities they serve, ensuring the work is getting done)? Don't we then have an obligation to steward our funds well and maximize the amount we can give to charities at the IRS's expense?

Let's explore some of the best ways to give to charity. We'll tackle five charitable gifting strategies, with examples, at least one of which you should be able to apply to your life. But first, let's ensure we understand what is currently deducible for charitable purposes.

The Deductibility of Charitable Gifts

"Aren't charitable gifts tax-deductible?"

Every charity advertises that you can make a "tax-deductible donation" to their cause. So do we even need strategies? Isn't it all just deductible?

No. It's not *all* necessarily deductible.

Let's review our tax return sequence.

Total Income The "Line"
- Adjustments* (Above-the-Line Deductions)
Adjusted Gross Income
- Standard OR Itemized Deductions (Below-the-Line)
Taxable Income
Nerd Note: *Adjustments include HSA/IRA contributions, Student Loan interest, some self-employment expenses, and other niche expenses.

Through 2025, charitable gifts were *only* deductible if you itemized deductions. Most couples do not have enough itemized deductions to exceed the standard deduction ($31,500 in 2025) and instead take the standard deduction. Thus, **while charitable gifts *are* tax-deductible, they are *not* deductible by most people.** (More on itemizing deductions in strategy two.)

Starting in 2026, all couples will be eligible for up to $2,000 in above-the-line deductions for charitable giving. This means that the first $2,000 you give to registered 501(c)(3) organizations will be deductible regardless of whether you itemize deductions or take the standard. Keep your year-end giving receipts from those charities for tax filing purposes.

(Note: All charitable gifting *tax* strategies involve giving to bona fide 501(c)(3) charities. These are typical charities, such as churches and the Red Cross. Giving cash to a homeless person or leaving a massive tip for a single-parent server at a restaurant are great acts, but they are never deductible.)

Since many of you are already donating or will eventually donate more than $2,000 annually, let's examine strategies to ensure the rest of your donations remain tax-deductible.

Qualified Charitable Distributions

You recall RMDs from chapters 1 and 4, correct? Required Minimum Distributions, those large chunks of money you will be forced to pull out of your pre-tax traditional IRAs after you reach your RMD age. They pose a significant problem for many, especially those who are not inclined to be charitable. But for the generous, there is a great strategy for turning the tables on the IRS.

The starting age for Required Minimum Distributions was 70 ½. In the year you turned 70 ½, the ending IRA balance of the previous year was used to determine your RMD. You had until tax day of the following year to take it out for that first year, and December 31st of every year after for subsequent RMDs.

Then, a couple of tax laws pushed the RMD age back to 72, and subsequently to either 73 (for those born between 1951 and 1959) or 75 (for those born in 1960 or later). Once you hit your RMD age, you must start taking distributions from your IRA of *at least* the prescribed amount, even if you don't want to. You can reinvest those funds in a brokerage account if you wish, but they must be withdrawn from your IRA at your highest marginal tax bracket, and they cannot be transferred into a Roth IRA via a conversion (see Chapter 4).

RMDs represent a tax tsunami coming for many. But there is some relief.

The Qualified Charitable Distribution (QCD) allows you to transfer money directly from your Traditional IRA to a charity and pay *zero* taxes on it. To qualify, you must be at least 70 ½ years old.

Rather than withdrawing money from an IRA, paying federal and state taxes on it, and then giving the net proceeds, you can give it directly from your custodian (Charles Schwab, Fidelity, Vanguard, etc.) to the charity.

Example: Bob & Sue's QCDs

Bob and Sue have been faithfully tithing 10% of their income, even in retirement. They are currently living off of $100,000 in gross Social Security income and pensions. They give $500 per month to their church and another $4,000 in chunks to various ministries throughout the year to reach their $10,000 annual goal.

Bob knows about his RMDs coming up at age 73. But he didn't realize that, while the RMD age had moved back, the QCD age remains 70 ½.

We switched Bob and Sue's giving strategy. We set up Qualified Charitable Distributions directly at Charles Schwab to send $2,000 directly to one of their consistent annual charities. Sue likes to "bring in the tithe" manually, so rather than mailing QCD checks directly, we set up a $500 monthly check made out to their church and mailed to them. Because they now get the $2,000 above-the-line charitable deduction, we left that amount in their giving budget for spontaneous giving. The result of these moves:

- They maintain charitable flexibility for some of their gifting.
- They are actively reducing their RMDs at 73.
- They convert $8,000 from taxable distributions to tax-free gifts, saving over $2,000/year in taxes.
- They will save more than $25,000 taxes over the next ten years from the QCDs, and an estimated $40,000 beyond that in reduced RMDs.

In the past, retirement account custodians such as Charles Schwab, Fidelity, and Vanguard lumped QCDs in with regular taxable retirement distributions on Form 1099-R (the form that reports retirement account distributions to the IRS and the taxpayer). A new provision in the 2025 tax law now allows custodians to issue a separate 1099-R for QCDs with the QCD designation. **Do not trust custodians to implement this correctly the first time.** Always double-check your tax forms to ensure your QCDs have not been mistakenly treated as taxable. It does no good to implement tax-savings strategies if a third party messes them up. Even if they successfully designate one year, re-check each year. Trust, but verify. Bob and Sue do not need to verify this, as we prepare and file their taxes and handle all the double-checks for them. Peace of mind plus less taxes equals a great retirement.

Deduction Bundling

Most people don't have enough deductions to itemize them beyond the Standard Deduction ($32,000** in 2026). But many are wasting their ability to itemize and paying extra taxes. **We can bundle deductions to take advantage of the tax code by alternating the years we itemize vs. taking the standard deduction.** Let's review itemized deductions, then look at an example to illustrate bundling.

Itemizable Deductions

Expenses eligible for itemized deductions are:

- Medical expenses in excess of 7.5% of AGI
- State and Local Taxes (SALT)
    - State Income Taxes
    - Property Taxes
    - Other local taxes based on your area
- Mortgage Interest (just the interest, not the principal)
- Gifts to Charity

Note: SALT used to be limited to $10,000/year. But the 2025 Tax Bill raised this cap to $40,000 for 2026 and beyond. This has dramatically increased the efficacy of deduction bundling.

Example: Steve & Rachel's Deduction Bundling

While Steve and Rachel have medical expenses, they do not come close to 7.5% of their AGI and cannot be itemized. Here are their annual itemized expenses over the past 2 years before working with us.

This Year Next Year

- State Income Tax: $7,000 $7,200

- Property Taxes: $5,000 $5,000
- Mortgage Interest: $6,000 $5,800
- Charitable Giving: $12,000 $12,000
- Total Itemizable: $30,000 $30,000
- Deduction Taken: Standard Standard
- "Wasted" Expenses: $30,000 $30,000

Because the Standard Deduction is $32,200 for 2026, they planned to take it and not itemize. That means they are "wasting" $30,000 in expenses that are technically deductible, but can't be claimed. Because they are paying down their mortgage and thus reducing their Mortgage Interest deduction, their itemized deductions will decline slightly next year, and they will waste those expenses as well. We showed them how they could bundle their deductions.

First, their annual property taxes are due in two installments: half on January 31st and half on July 31st, but they receive their property tax bill in late November for the following year. They've always paid it on the due dates. But this year, we plan to pay this year's taxes on time, *and* **next year's in December.** That bundles two years of taxes into one. Taxes are itemizable when they are paid, not when they are due.

Second, we are going to **give all of next year's giving this year**. We'll let their church and charities know this is an advanced lump-sum gift this year, in place of monthly giving next year, so that they can budget accordingly. We are effectively giving the same amount over two years, but bundling it into one year. Let's look at the effect of these two moves:

This Year Next Year

- State Income Tax: $7,000 $7,200
- Property Taxes: **$10,000 $0**

- Mortgage Interest: $6,000 $5,800
- Charitable Giving: **$24,000 $0**
- Total Itemizable: $47,000 $13,000
- Deduction Taken: Itemized Standard
- "Wasted" Expenses: $0 $13,000

They are now $15,000 over the Standard Deduction this year and can itemize instead. Further, they would have been under the threshold next year anyway, but we are reducing the amount of "wasted" expenses next year and still allowing them to itemize. Assuming the Standard deduction is $33,000 next year, we went from $65,000 in deductions over two years to $80,000.

While many tax savings "strategies" (such as IRA contributions and purchasing insurance products) claim to save you taxes, in reality, they are just kicking the can down the road, and sometimes having you pay *more* taxes overall. **Deduction bundling provides true tax savings with no additional out-of-pocket costs and no additional taxes later.** It's not a matter of *if* Steve and Rachel will have these expenses; it's a matter of when. They are going to pay them either way. But by simply moving *when* they pay them up a few months, *they save $4,400 in taxes*. Furthermore, they can repeat this strategy every other year, *saving them over $22,000 in taxes over the next decade with no additional out-of-pocket costs.*

Gifting Appreciated Investments

If you have a brokerage account (see Chapter 5), listen up. Many people have investments in a brokerage account that have grown significantly since they bought them. If these stocks, mutual funds, or ETFs are sold inside the brokerage account, the owner will pay long-term capital gains taxes on the difference between what they paid and the sale price.

Furthermore, while capital gains don't count toward your ordinary income tax bracket, they do count in your Adjusted Gross Income, which counts toward several other limits and deductions. Thus, many people hold positions longer than they should because they don't want to pay taxes. They are also giving inefficiently to charity. Herein lies the tax strategy.

You can give highly appreciated investments directly to charity without selling them. You receive the fair market value as a charitable deduction, *and* **you pay no taxes on the sale of the investment.** The charity can sell the investment and will pay no tax on it under its 501(c) (3) tax exemption. Let's look at this in an example.

Example: Steve & Rachel's High Growth ETF

Steve & Rachel loved the idea of Deduction Bundling, but weren't sure they could come up with all of next year's taxes and gifting up front. With busy lives, they are cash-flowing most expenses. And while they *could* dip into their emergency fund, they don't consider this an emergency.

However, they are regularly funding a brokerage account as part of their retirement. Inside that brokerage account is Vanguard's Growth ETF with the ticker VUG. It has appreciated nicely over the last decade, but may not continue to outperform as the winds of change blow.

We recommended that they stop giving to charity this year out of cash flow. Rather, let's give all of this year's *and* next year's charity, $24,000, by gifting it now with VUG stock. We'll tax-optimize by choosing the earliest purchases of the stock with the lowest cost basis (amount paid for the investment) and therefore the highest growth.

They have $24,000's worth of the ETF, for which they paid a combined $4,000. If they sold the stock, they'd have a $20,000 gain and owe 15% in capital gains taxes. Because of their income, they'd *also* owe Net Investment Income Tax (NIIT) of 3.8% on it. That's over $3,600 in taxes, leaving them with just over $20,000 if they sold. But by giving the appreciated stock, they cannot only take advantage of the $4,400 Deduction Bundling strategy but *also* save $3,600 in investment taxes. **Through proper tax savings strategies, Steve & Rachel will save over $8,000 in taxes this year with nothing out of pocket: pure tax savings.**

Because this brokerage account is for retirement, we'll use the cash flow they previously had allocated to charity and property taxes over the next two years to contribute back to the brokerage account, dollar-cost-averaging the market volatility and resetting their cost basis for future tax savings.

Gifting appreciated investments can be a tremendous way to save taxes, especially when combined with deduction bunding.

Donor Advised Funds

What if you have a large sum of money you want earmarked for gifting, but you don't want to gift it all at once? That's where a Donor Advised Fund comes in handy.

A Donor Advised Fund (DAF) is a charitable fund that allows you to donate funds now for the current charitable tax benefits, but then keep it invested in the fund for future disbursements. The money keeps growing according to the general strategy you desire, and you can choose which charities you want the fund to make donations to. It's a great way to give now and spread out donations across time.

Populare Donor Advised Funds we use are Charles Schwab's DAFgiving360 and Fidelity Charitable.

Example: Chuck & Diane's Inheritance

Diane's mother passed away, leaving a home and some assets to Diane and her two siblings. After selling the home, Diane receives $130,000 as an inheritance. They give some to their children, but still have $100,000 they don't plan to spend immediately. They don't need it for retirement, and investing it in a brokerage account will only add extra taxes and more money that they don't need.

Chuck and Diane like the idea of deduction bundling, but without a mortgage, they are even further from being able to itemize than Steve and Rachel. We also plan to do Qualified Charitable Distributions with them in the future, but at 60 years old, we are a ways out from being able to do that. They give about $15,000 per year to their church and charities, and are currently doing it out of IRA distributions.

We recommended they contribute the $100,000 to a Donor Advised Fund. We'll also pull next years $5,000 property tax into this year to bundle it. This gives them an Itemized Deduction of $113,000 this year, $81,000 in additional deductions over their Standard Deduction. *That will save them over $22,000 in taxes this year.* Beyond that, they can direct their annual giving from the DAF, which should provide the next seven years of gifting without taxable distributions. The tax savings break down like this:

Event Amount Tax Savings

- Year 1 *Extra* Deductions: $81,000 $22,100
- Year 1-7 IRA distributions: $15,000/y $4,100/y
- Total Tax Savings: $50,700

By correctly using this $100,000 inheritance, Chuck and Diane will **save $50,000 in taxes over the next seven years**, true tax savings with nothing additional out of pocket.

Legacy Giving

Most charitable giving strategies focus on what you give during life. But for many couples over fifty, one of the most powerful charitable strategies happens at death.

If you already know you want to leave a portion of your estate to your church or favorite charities, the question is not *whether* to give, but how. The question is **which assets should go to whom**.

Not all dollars are created equal in the eyes of the IRS.

Bob & Sue's Charitable Legacy

Bob and Sue have been faithful givers for decades. They tithe regularly and support several ministries. They also know that when both of them pass away, they would like 10% of their remaining estate to go to their church and a few charities that have meant a lot to their family.

On the surface, the simplest approach would be to write that into their will or trust:

"Upon our death, 10% of our estate goes to charity, and the remainder goes equally to our children."

That sounds clean. But it is not tax-efficient.

Bob and Sue's balance sheet includes:

- Traditional IRAs (pre-tax money)
- Roth IRAs (tax-free money)
- A brokerage account (eligible for a step-up in basis)
- Some savings and home equity

If they leave 10% of everything proportionally, their children will inherit some of the Traditional IRA.

And that is where the tax inefficiency begins.

Why Pre-Tax IRAs Are the Worst Asset to Leave to Children

Under current law, when children inherit a Traditional IRA, they must empty the account within 10 years. Every dollar withdrawn is taxed as ordinary income at *their* tax rate.

If Bob and Sue's children are in their peak earning years, those inherited IRA withdrawals could be taxed at 24%, 32%, or even higher when state taxes are included.

In other words, a $100,000 inherited Traditional IRA might only produce $65,000–$75,000 of after-tax value for their children.

But here is the key insight:

Charities do not pay income taxes.

If a 501(c)(3) charity inherits a Traditional IRA, it can withdraw 100% of the funds with no tax due. No ordinary income tax. No 10-year distribution burden. No tax drag.

That same $100,000 IRA produces the full $100,000 benefit to the charity.

So if Bob and Sue want to give $100,000 to charity at death, it is dramatically more efficient to give it from their pre-tax IRA than from other assets.

The Optimal Asset Location at Death

Instead of naming charities in their will for a percentage of the estate, Bob and Sue can:

- Name their church and charities as beneficiaries of a portion of their **Traditional IRAs**
- Leave their **Roth IRAs and brokerage accounts to their children**

This accomplishes several powerful tax outcomes:

1. **Charity receives pre-tax IRA dollars completely tax-free.**
2. **Children avoid inheriting heavily taxed Traditional IRA assets.**
3. **Children inherit Roth IRAs**, which:
    - Continue growing tax-free for up to 10 years.
    - Can be withdrawn tax-free at any point within that 10-year window.
4. **Children inherit brokerage assets with a full step-up in basis**, eliminating capital gains on lifetime appreciation.

That is strategic generosity. The IRS gets less. The charity gets more. The children keep more.

Beneficiary Strategies are Superior to Estate Docs

Many people assume estate planning documents are the proper place to handle charitable giving. While wills and trusts are essential, they are not the most tax-efficient tool for directing retirement assets.

Retirement accounts pass by **beneficiary designation**, not by will.

If Bob and Sue simply say in their will, "Give $100,000 to charity," the executor may need to pull money proportionally from all accounts. That could mean:

- Liquidating brokerage assets (losing the step-up opportunity).
- Distributing Roth dollars (which are the most tax-advantaged asset to heirs).
- Or unnecessarily burdening the children with inherited pre-tax dollars.

By contrast, updating beneficiary designations:

- Is simple.
- Is free.
- Requires no attorney fees.
- Can be changed at any time.

If Bob and Sue change their minds about which charity to support, they can fill out a new beneficiary form with Schwab, Fidelity, or Vanguard. No legal documents need to be redrafted. No trust amendments. No cost.

Beneficiary forms override wills. That makes them incredibly powerful—and incredibly important to review regularly.

The Big Picture

Charitable giving at death is not just about generosity. It is about **asset location at death**, just like we discussed asset location in Chapter 5 for investments.

The general rule for charitably inclined couples is:

- Leave **pre-tax dollars** to charity.

- Leave **Roth dollars and step-up eligible assets** to children.

When done properly, this strategy can:

- Increase what the charity receives.
- Increase what children receive.
- Reduce lifetime family taxes.
- And require no additional giving during life.

It is one of the rare strategies where everyone wins—except the IRS.

If you are already planning to give at death, make sure you are giving the right dollars to the right people.

That is not just generosity.

That is tax-smart generosity.

The Charitable Challenge

Let me ask you a simple question.

If the market dropped 10% the month before you passed away, and your children inherited 10% less than expected, would they be okay? For most of you reading this book, the honest answer is yes. It might not be ideal, but it would not derail their lives, their retirements, or their financial security.

If your children would be okay with a 10% market decline, why not consider a 10% charitable designation?

Instead of allowing market volatility to determine that outcome randomly, you could determine it intentionally. You could name your church and favorite charities as beneficiaries of 10% of your net worth—funded entirely from your pre-tax IRA accounts. That 10% would go to causes that advance the Kingdom, serve your community, and reflect your values, while your children inherit Roth assets and step-up-in-basis brokerage accounts in a far more tax-efficient way.

A market drop is an accidental reduction. A beneficiary designation is intentional generosity.

If you are charitably inclined, I challenge you to review your IRA beneficiary forms this month. Consider allocating 10% of your total investment balance in those pre-tax accounts directly to the churches and charities you love. You might need to calculate an odd percentage for your IRAs to encapsulate your total balance, but the math is simple. Your children will likely be just fine—and your legacy will be larger than money alone.

Chapter Summary
- Charitable giving is not just about generosity—it is about intentional tax planning that allows you to give more while paying less to the IRS.
- Charitable gifts are only deductible if you itemize, but beginning in 2026, up to $2,000 of giving will be available as an above-the-line deduction for all couples.
- Qualified Charitable Distributions (QCDs) allow you to give directly from a Traditional IRA after age 70½ and avoid recognizing the income entirely—reducing taxes, lowering AGI, and shrinking future RMDs.
- Deduction bundling allows you to alternate between itemizing and taking the standard deduction by consolidating charitable gifts and certain expenses into a single tax year, creating real tax savings with no additional lifetime cost.
- Gifting appreciated investments avoids capital gains taxes while still providing a full fair-market-value charitable deduction.
- Donor Advised Funds allow you to front-load deductions in high-income years while spreading grants to charities over time.
- Naming charities as beneficiaries of pre-tax IRAs is often the most tax-efficient way to leave a legacy, while Roth IRAs

and step-up-in-basis brokerage assets are generally better left to children.
- Strategic generosity increases what your church or charity receives, increases what your children keep, and reduces what goes to the IRS.

Action Items

1. Review your annual giving. Are you giving from cash flow when a QCD, appreciated stock gift, or bundling strategy would be more efficient?
2. If you are age 70½ or older, contact your IRA custodian and ask about setting up Qualified Charitable Distributions before taking taxable withdrawals.
3. Evaluate whether deduction bundling could allow you to itemize every other year. Look specifically at property taxes and charitable giving timing.
4. Review your brokerage account for highly appreciated positions that could be gifted directly instead of sold.
5. If you receive a large inheritance, bonus, or liquidity event, consider whether a Donor Advised Fund would allow you to capture a large deduction in a high-income year.
6. Pull out your IRA beneficiary forms this month. Consider designating a percentage of pre-tax IRA assets directly to your church or favorite charities.
7. Coordinate beneficiary designations with your estate documents to ensure the right assets are going to the right people in the most tax-efficient way.

Generosity is already part of your life. These strategies simply ensure that when you give, you are doing so in a way that maximizes impact, minimizes unnecessary taxes, and reflects both your values and your wisdom.

Legacy Tax Planning

Chapter 8
Minimizing Taxes for the Next Generation

One of the most useful principles from *The 7 Habits of Highly Effective People* is also one of the most neglected principles in retirement planning: **Begin with the end in mind.** Most of this book has focused on your lifetime taxes—how you and your spouse can keep more of what you've earned, reduce hidden marginal rates, and avoid accidental tax traps.

But there is a second layer to tax planning that matters just as much: **legacy taxes.** When you are gone, who will pay the taxes? What kind of money will they inherit—pre-tax, tax-free, or taxable? How quickly will they be forced to take distributions? And how much of your wealth will get skimmed off at the worst possible time—during grief, paperwork, and transition?

Legacy tax planning is not morbid. It is practical.

If taxes are your largest lifetime expense, then legacy taxes are often your family's largest "one-time" expense. The good news is that many of these taxes are optional. They are not optional in the sense that you can ignore the IRS, but optional in the sense that you can **choose better account types, better timing, and better beneficiary strategies** while you are alive.

That's what this chapter is all about.

Limiting the Widow Tax

This section is all about what I call **the Widow Tax**—the painful reality that when one spouse dies, the surviving spouse typically keeps most of the income and nearly all of the assets, but loses half of the tax brackets.

If you have ever heard someone say, "Taxes will be lower when one of us is gone because there's only one person," please take that thought and throw it away. Yes, there is one person, but the tax code doesn't politely adjust to that reality.

What Is the Widow Tax?

The Widow Tax occurs when a couple goes from **Married Filing Jointly** to **Single** status. In general, many key tax thresholds get cut in half. That includes ordinary income tax brackets, capital gains brackets, and several "extra tax" thresholds, such as IRMAA and (often) the Net Investment Income Tax.

Meanwhile, real life does not cut in half.

The survivor still lives in the same house. Property taxes don't decline because you have fewer people on the couch. Insurance premiums and home maintenance don't magically become 50% cheaper. You may drive less, but you're still driving the same vehicle, maintaining the same property, and paying many of the same fixed expenses.

Income also often stays surprisingly high. The survivor does not lose "half" of the household income in most cases. They often lose some income, but keep the largest parts, and the income they keep is now forced into a smaller tax bracket structure.

The Widow Tax is most severe when:

- There is a meaningful age gap between spouses.
- One spouse has significantly better health or family longevity.
- A pension includes survivor benefits.
- The household has large pre-tax IRA balances and future RMDs.
- The couple has already delayed tax planning, leaving the survivor "stuck" with big required distributions.

In other words, the Widow Tax often shows up for the people who did everything "responsibly": saved diligently, built large retirement accounts, and created a secure retirement. It's just that security can produce a different problem.

Social Security Impacts

Social Security survivor benefits are one of the clearest examples of income that is not cut in half.

When one spouse dies, the survivor generally receives **the larger of the two Social Security checks** (not both). This means the household may lose one check, but often keeps the bigger one. If the higher-earning spouse delayed Social Security and the lower-earning spouse claimed early, the survivor benefit can be especially large relative to what they were used to.

So what happens to taxes?

The survivor keeps the larger benefit, and their other income sources may also remain similar. But the tax brackets are now single, and the survivor's **Provisional Income** is often higher relative to the (unchanged) Social Security taxability thresholds.

This produces a double effect:

- The survivor may have **a higher percentage of Social Security become taxable**, and

- The survivor pays that tax in **tighter tax brackets**.

The result is that Social Security can feel "more taxable" even if the gross benefit did not collapse.

Pension Impacts

Pensions are another major reason the Widow Tax happens.

Most people elect some form of survivor benefit when they retire with a pension. Sometimes it's 100%. Often it's 66⅔% or 75%. Regardless, most pensions do not get cut in half at the first death.

From a planning perspective, this is usually a good decision. Losing a pension entirely would be financially devastating. The problem is not the survivor benefit. The problem is that the survivor benefit keeps taxable income relatively high, while the tax brackets shrink.

So pensions can turn the Widow Tax from an inconvenience into a multi-year drag.

IRA and Asset Impacts

This is typically the biggest driver.

For most couples, household retirement assets do not get cut in half when the first spouse dies. In most cases, the surviving spouse is the 100% primary beneficiary on the retirement accounts. That means the IRA or 401(k) balance simply rolls to the survivor.

The survivor still has the same account value. They still have the same future Required Minimum Distributions. And those RMDs are now taxed in single brackets.

This is where the Widow Tax becomes predictable.

If you want to estimate the severity, ask:

- "How big will our pre-tax accounts be when RMDs start?"
- "What will our RMDs look like at 73, 75, 80, 85?"
- "What happens if one of us is single for 5–10 years?"

A retirement plan that looks tax-efficient for the couple can become tax-expensive for the survivor, not because the survivor made bad decisions, but because the tax code is less forgiving.

Examples of the Widow Tax

Let's make this tangible using our case study couples.

Example 1: Bob & Sue (moderate income)

Assume Bob passes at age 85 and Sue passes at age 92. That's eight years Sue will file as Single.

Let's assume that, with good planning, Bob and Sue can keep their taxable income under roughly $100,000 (in 2026 dollars) and stay in the 12% bracket when filing MFJ. That might be their "comfort zone." They're not trying to hit home runs. They want a stable retirement income with steady taxes.

Now fast-forward.

When Sue is single, the tax brackets are effectively cut in half. That means the same taxable income that lived comfortably in the 12% bracket as a couple can push her into the 22% bracket as a widow.

If Sue pays roughly $11,000 per year in federal income taxes as part of the couple, she might now pay roughly $17,000 per year as a widow on a similar level of taxable income. That is about a **54% increase.**

Over eight years, that's almost **$50,000** in extra taxes.

That $50,000 is Sue's Widow Tax.

Example 2: Chuck & Diane (higher income)

Assume Chuck passes at age 85 and Diane passes at age 92. Again, that's eight years Diane will file as Single.

Chuck and Diane are targeting the 22% bracket as a couple. In 2026 dollars, that might mean keeping taxable income around $211,000 or less. But let's say unmanaged RMDs push them toward $250,000 per year and into the 24% bracket while MFJ.

Now Diane becomes single.

As a widow, $210,000 of taxable income sits in the **middle of the 32% bracket**, and $257,000 can push her into the **35% bracket**.

She may not want or need to spend $257,000. That doesn't matter. RMDs don't ask what you need.

On top of that, the thresholds for **NIIT** and **IRMAA** are much easier to trigger as a single filer. Diane may now face:

- Federal income tax at a far higher marginal bracket
- NIIT adding an extra 3.8% on investment income
- Higher IRMAA tiers increasing Medicare Part B and D premiums NOW based on income two years ago.

In a simplified illustration, Chuck & Diane might owe around $45,200 in federal income tax and $1,900 in IRMAA as a couple, while Diane might owe around $56,500 in federal income tax and $4,400 in IRMAA as a widow.

That's roughly **$13,800 per year** in extra taxes and premiums.

Over eight years, that's about **$110,000**.

That $110,000 is Diane's Widow Tax.

Do you see the pattern?

The Widow Tax is not a theoretical planning concept. It's the predictable result of large pre-tax retirement accounts colliding with smaller tax brackets.

How to Solve for the Widow Tax

For most couples, **RMDs are the accelerant** that turns the Widow Tax into a wildfire.

That doesn't mean RMDs are "bad." It means that if your pre-tax accounts are large and you haven't been proactive, RMDs can force taxable income higher than you would otherwise choose.

The typical solution is a strategy you already know from Chapter 4:

- **Aggressive, early Roth conversions**

The goal is not to avoid taxes. The goal is to **choose when and at what rate you pay them.**

A good Widow Tax plan often looks like this:

1. In early retirement (often before Social Security and before Medicare IRMAA becomes a concern), intentionally convert to Roth.
2. Temporarily and proactively use some of the next tax bracket.
3. Reduce the future size of RMDs.
4. Reduce the chance that the survivor gets pushed up multiple brackets.

This is one of the rare times when I will tell you that it can make sense to "pay more taxes now" in order to pay less later.

And because you are planning as a couple, you can model it realistically:

- Plan a large gap in death ages.
- Stress-test the survivor's tax return.
- Run IRMAA and NIIT scenarios.
- Build a conversion plan that's designed for the survivor, not just for the couple.

Finally, remember the account types:

- **Roth accounts are never a concern.** They don't create RMD pressure in the same way, and inherited Roths can grow tax-free.
- **Correctly titled brokerage assets may create a step-up in basis** at death (more on that later), which can make the survivor's investment taxes easier to manage.

If you want to protect your spouse, don't just plan for "us." Plan for "the last one standing."

Generational Taxes

Once we've addressed the Widow Tax, we need to zoom out to a broader question: **What happens after both of you are gone?**

You may be doing an excellent job of minimizing taxes over your lifetime and still end up accidentally leaving your children a tax mess.

This isn't because you failed.

It's because the tax code treats inherited pre-tax retirement accounts in a very specific way, and the timing often collides with the peak earning years of your children.

The Conundrum

Here is the basic reality:

- You may live into your late eighties or nineties.
- Your children may be in their late fifties or sixties when they inherit.
- They likely have their own retirement plan and tax plan.

Then, suddenly, they inherit hundreds of thousands—or millions—of dollars.

If a large portion of that inheritance is in pre-tax retirement accounts, the kids have to distribute those accounts according to the current inherited IRA rules. For many heirs, this means the money must be distributed within 10 years.

That's not an "income stream." That's a forced tax event.

If your kids are already in their higher earning years, inherited IRA distributions can:

- Push them into higher brackets
- Trigger NIIT on investment income
- Trigger IRMAA surcharges once they are on Medicare
- Increase taxation of their own Social Security later

In other words, you may have done decades of careful planning only to have the inheritance taxed at the highest rate possible.

This is why legacy planning must be done from the beginning with the end in mind.

Options for Reducing Generational Taxes

There are many ways to reduce generational taxes. Most of them are not complicated. They just require intentionality.

Below are four core options. Notice that they are not mutually exclusive. Many couples do a blend of multiple strategies.

1) Give More to Charity

If you are charitably inclined, this may be the cleanest legacy tax strategy available.

Charities do not pay income tax. If a qualified charity inherits a Traditional IRA, they can receive that money without paying taxes on it. That means **the most tax-heavy assets you own can be the most efficient assets to leave to charity.**

This is why the beneficiary designation strategy in Chapter 7 is so powerful.

If you plan to give a meaningful portion of your estate to churches and charities at death, it often makes sense to earmark:

- Pre-tax IRAs and 401(k)s for charity
- Roth and brokerage assets for children

That one decision can shift tens of thousands—or hundreds of thousands—of dollars away from the IRS.

There's also a psychological advantage.

If you plan to give to charity at death, consider giving more during life. You get to see the impact. You get to enjoy the mission. You may get to watch your generosity change real lives.

You can still leave something behind, but you'll have fewer "unknowns" at death.

2) Give More to Children Now

Most people do not want to create trust-fund babies. That's not what we're talking about.

We're talking about recognizing something simple:

If you have responsible children, they probably will not "need" an inheritance at age 65.

But many adult children go through what I call **the pinch**—a season where life is expensive, income is still ramping up, and the family is stretched thin. Common pinch markers include:

- Young kids with either a single income or high daycare costs
- Early career years with a lower income relative to later years
- Higher mortgage payment relative to income, without home equity to lean on

In this season, a well-timed gift can have a disproportionate impact.

A gift might look like:

- Helping with a down payment
- Paying off a high-interest student loan
- Funding a "memory-making" family vacation
- Covering a season of daycare so one spouse can breathe

This can also reduce future generational taxes. When you give while you are alive, you can often give under the annual gift exclusion rules, and you can choose timing that aligns with your own tax plan.

One important caution: don't give in a way that compromises your retirement. The goal is to help without creating new dependencies or jeopardizing your own plan.

3) Spend More on Yourself

This is not a joke.

Many couples retire with the mindset that they must preserve assets at all costs. Then, thirty years later, they die with three to five times what they started with.

That is not "bad." It's just that it often creates the generational tax conundrum.

If your goal is to maximize after-tax wealth, remember that the "after-tax" part applies to your children, too.

If you have more than enough, it may make sense to:

- Enjoy more of your money while you are alive
- Spend down pre-tax accounts intentionally
- Preserve Roth and brokerage assets for legacy

This is why a good retirement plan includes *permission.*
Permission to spend.
Permission to travel.
Permission to buy the camper.
Permission to give the grandkids an experience.

Because the alternative can be leaving them a tax bill instead of a blessing.

4) Do More Roth Conversions

Here's the generational Roth conversion argument:

Your children may inherit your IRA during their highest tax years.

If they are going to pay 32%–37% (plus state tax) to liquidate an inherited IRA, and you can pay 12%–24% now to convert it to Roth, then you might be doing them a favor.

Even if your bracket and theirs are "similar," converting now still gives you advantages:

- You control the timing.
- You avoid the forced 10-year inheritance window.
- You reduce the odds of NIIT and IRMAA stacking for your kids.

A Roth conversion strategy can also give you tax-controllable money for giving and spending later.

That said, Roth conversions should never be done blindly.

If you plan to leave most of your IRA to charity, then converting those dollars to Roth may be unnecessary. Why pay taxes now on money a charity would receive tax-free later?

This is exactly why we began the chapter with the end in mind.

Inheritance Strategies

Legacy planning isn't only about what you leave. Many of you will also inherit.

Couples over fifty often inherit from parents in their eighties and nineties. That means you may receive an inheritance during your own retirement planning years, or even during your own early retirement.

This section includes strategies you can employ if you inherit, and strategies your heirs can employ when they inherit from you.

Inherited IRAs

Inherited IRAs are one of the most common "surprise tax problems" in retirement.

Under current rules for many non-spouse beneficiaries, inherited retirement accounts often must be fully distributed by the end of year ten after death. Depending on the year of death and the beneficiary type, there may also be annual distribution requirements along the way.

Regardless of the exact rules that apply to you, one planning principle remains consistent:

It is usually a bad plan to take only the smallest amount possible for nine years and then take a massive lump sum in year ten.

That approach can create a tax cliff.

Instead, good inherited IRA planning asks:

- "What bracket am I in each of the next ten years?"
- "Do I have any low-income years coming up?"
- "Could I intentionally distribute more in years where my income is lower?"
- "Can I avoid pushing myself into the highest bracket in year ten?"

This doesn't mean you take the exact same amount each year. Life isn't that tidy.

But it does mean you should plan a range and sequence.

If you are still working, you might distribute less now and more later. If you retire in three years, you might distribute more after retirement when your earned income drops. If you are close to Medicare, you might keep a close eye on IRMAA thresholds.

An inherited IRA is a decade-long planning opportunity. Don't treat it like a tax form.

Inherited Roth IRAs

Inherited Roth IRAs are the opposite.

If you inherit a Roth IRA, and you are not required to take annual distributions, you should strongly consider letting that money compound for the full ten years and then withdrawing it at the end—tax-free.

The inherited Roth IRA may be one of the most powerful wealth-building assets you ever touch. It is tax-free compounding on someone else's work.

The biggest risk is that heirs treat it like "free money" and invest it like a checking account.

If your heirs inherit a Roth IRA, encourage them to:

- Invest it for growth (within their risk tolerance)
- Let it compound for as long as the rules allow
- Plan the final withdrawal intentionally

This is a great place to point them to *3D Retirement Income*. The investment philosophy matters here. If they invest the inherited Roth conservatively, it will remain stable. If they invest it thoughtfully for long-term growth, they can multiply the blessing.

Non-Qualified Accounts

Brokerage accounts are often the most "inheritance-friendly" asset class from a tax perspective because of the **step-up in basis** rules.

When someone dies, many taxable brokerage assets receive a new cost basis based on the value at death. That means heirs may be able to sell shortly after inheriting with little to no capital gains tax.

This creates two practical strategies.

First, if the heirs want a different investment allocation, inheritance can be a great time to reposition.

Second, heirs should pay attention to timing.

If you inherit a brokerage account and immediately reinvest according to your long-term plan, you are likely fine. But if you leave it untouched for months, and then sell a year later, you might accidentally create:

- Short-term capital gains (taxed as ordinary income) if you sell new purchases too soon
- A delay that forces you to hold a full year for long-term capital gains on any post-inheritance growth

In other words, inheritance is a perfect time to make clean moves. Don't let uncertainty create tax sloppiness.

Finally, remember a strategy from Chapter 7: using a Donor Advised Fund.

If you inherit and also want to accelerate Roth conversions, realize capital gains, or fund a major tax strategy, charitable tools can help offset the tax impact in the same year.

Inheritance years can be high-income years. Plan accordingly.

Other Inheritance Strategies

Here are a few additional legacy planning ideas that don't fit neatly in a single account type.

1) Review beneficiaries immediately.

If a spouse dies, the surviving spouse should update beneficiaries immediately. If you don't, assets can accidentally flow to outdated beneficiaries, minor children, or even the estate itself, creating probate and tax complications.

2) Know which assets are "income tax bombs."

Traditional IRAs and 401(k)s are income tax bombs for heirs. Roth accounts are not. Brokerage accounts can be tax-light due to step-up. If you know which assets are heavy, you can plan the order of inheritance.

3) Coordinate with your kids' tax plan.

This sounds obvious, but many families never talk about it. If your children are high earners, inherited IRA planning becomes even more critical. If they will retire soon, the ideal distribution schedule may be entirely different.

4) Don't accidentally leave a mess for your executor.

A great estate plan is clear. Clear titling, clear beneficiary designations, clean account lists, and good records reduce both tax errors and family stress.

Legacy planning is not just taxes. It is mercy.

Estate Taxes

When people hear "legacy taxes," many immediately think about estate taxes—sometimes called "death taxes" or "inheritance taxes." Those terms get mixed up constantly, so let's separate them.

- **Estate taxes** are taxes on the estate itself before assets pass to heirs.
- **Inheritance taxes** are taxes paid by the heir who receives the assets.

The federal system is an estate tax system. Several states also impose estate taxes, and a smaller group impose inheritance taxes.

What Are Estate Taxes?

Federal estate tax applies only when an estate exceeds the federal exemption amount.

For 2026, the federal exemption is extremely high: roughly **$15,000,000 per person** (about **$30,000,000** for a married couple with portability in play). Above that exemption, the federal estate tax rate can be up to 40%.

For most families reading this book, the federal estate tax is not the primary issue.

But that doesn't mean "estate taxes don't matter." Two things can still make them relevant.

First, you might live in a state with its own estate tax.

Second, you might be surprised how quickly an estate can grow.

I have worked with clients who enter retirement with assets in the low millions and assume estate tax isn't a concern. Then we project out 20–30 years with:

- Steady market growth
- Real estate appreciation
- One spouse dying and the survivor spending less

Suddenly, the estate is far larger than expected.

The message is not "be afraid." The message is "project it."

State estate taxes

Some states have estate tax thresholds that are dramatically lower than the federal exemption.

For example, Minnesota has an estate tax system. That means a family could be nowhere near federal estate tax territory and still owe state estate tax, depending on their total assets and the state's exemption.

This matters because it is easy to think:

"Federal exemption is huge, so we're fine."

But for some states, "fine" is a much smaller number.

Strategies for Minimizing Estate Taxes

If your projected estate could be subject to state estate tax—or in rare cases, federal estate tax—there are strategies to consider.

Some are "clean," and some are complex. The goal of this book is not to make you an estate attorney. The goal is to help you know what levers exist so you can ask better questions.

1) Know your state rules—and consider relocation cautiously

Moving to a different state can reduce or eliminate state estate taxes.

That said, moving "for taxes" rarely works if you only look at one tax. Many no-estate-tax states have other taxes that may be higher (property tax, sales tax, insurance costs, etc.). If you are considering relocation, evaluate the full tax landscape, healthcare access, and family proximity.

If you were already planning to move, the estate tax system may become one more data point in the decision.

2) Use the marital deduction correctly

Most couples avoid estate tax at the first death because transfers to a spouse are generally deductible for estate tax purposes.

That sounds great—until you realize it can simply push the entire problem onto the second death.

A common objective in estate planning is to ensure both spouses' exemptions can be used effectively, especially at the state level, where exemptions may not be portable.

This is where certain trust structures can matter, but even without a complex structure, good beneficiary planning and titling can help.

3) Consider disclaimer planning

A disclaimer is a legal refusal of an inheritance.

That sounds strange, but it can be a powerful planning tool.

For example, a surviving spouse might disclaim part of an inheritance so it passes to a trust or to children, using an exemption that would otherwise be wasted. Disclaimers are technical and must follow strict timing and control rules.

But the big idea is simple:

Sometimes the best plan is one that gives your family options.

4) Use lifetime gifting strategically

Lifetime gifting can reduce the taxable estate.

At the federal level, you can give up to the annual exclusion amount per recipient per year without using your lifetime exemption. In 2026, the annual exclusion is $19,000 per recipient (or $38,000 per couple).

This means a couple with three adult children and six grandchildren could potentially move meaningful money out of the estate over time without touching the lifetime exemption.

If larger gifting is needed, the lifetime exemption is still available. But at that point, you are firmly in "estate attorney" territory, and you should coordinate carefully.

5) Use irrevocable strategies only when the math demands it

Some estate tax strategies involve irrevocable trusts and life insurance structures designed to provide liquidity at death.

These can be appropriate for truly large estates where estate tax is unavoidable, and liquidity planning is important.

But remember Chapter 3.

Life insurance and complex products are often sold under the banner of "tax savings" when they do not actually save taxes, or when the costs exceed the benefits. If you need a complex estate solution, it should be because the math demands it—not because someone is selling you an idea.

A good professional will show you the numbers, trade-offs, and alternatives.

Beginning With the End in Mind

Legacy tax planning forces you to think differently.

Instead of asking, "How do we pay the least taxes this year?" you begin asking:

- "What will our survivor pay?"
- "What will our kids pay?"
- "What kind of money are we leaving behind?"
- "What tax rules will hit them at the worst possible time?"

The Widow Tax is often the first domino. Then come generational taxes, inherited IRA rules, and state estate taxes.

Hundreds of thousands of dollars can be at stake. For some families, it's not just dollars—it's optionality, generosity, and a smoother transition for the next generation.

And yes, this kind of planning requires thinking, modeling, and integrating multiple parts of the plan.

If that feels overwhelming, you are not alone.

This is why Chapter 10 exists.

Tax planning is powerful, but it is also detailed. Many readers start this book excited—then feel fatigue once the strategies and thresholds pile up. If you feel that happening, don't quit. Skip ahead to Chapter 10 and read the section on Financial Fatigue and working with a tax strategist.

Begin with the end in mind—and then take the next right step.

Chapter Summary

- **The Widow Tax is real and predictable.** When one spouse dies, tax brackets, IRMAA thresholds, and other income limits shrink—while income and assets often do not. Without proactive planning, the survivor can be pushed into significantly higher marginal tax brackets.
- **RMDs are often the accelerant.** Large pre-tax accounts combined with single-filing status can result in years of avoidable over-taxation. Strategic Roth conversions earlier in retirement are often the cleanest solution.
- **Generational taxes can undo good lifetime planning.** Inherited IRAs distributed over ten years can collide with your children's highest earning years, increasing their marginal rates, NIIT exposure, and Medicare premiums later.
- **Account type matters at death.** Traditional IRAs are income-tax-heavy for heirs. Roth IRAs are income-tax-free. Brokerage accounts may receive a step-up in basis. The mix you leave behind determines how much of your wealth goes to family versus the IRS.
- **Estate taxes are not a problem for most—but projections matter.** Federal exemptions are high, but some states have much lower thresholds. Long-term compounding can

quietly move families into estate tax territory if nothing changes.

Legacy planning is not about hoarding wealth. It is about directing it wisely. With intentional modeling and coordinated strategy, many of these taxes can be reduced, deferred, or eliminated.

Action Items

If this chapter stirred questions, that's a good sign. Here are practical next steps to begin implementing legacy-aware tax planning:

1. **Model the Widow Scenario.**
   Ask your advisor (or run your own projections), assuming one spouse dies 5–10 years before the other. Compare the couple's projected taxes with the survivor's projected taxes. Identify the Widow Tax gap.
2. **Project Future RMDs.**
   Estimate your pre-tax account balances at ages 73, 75, 80, and 85. Calculate projected RMDs and evaluate whether they will push the survivor into higher brackets.
3. **Review Beneficiary Designations.**
   Confirm primary and contingent beneficiaries on every retirement and brokerage account. Make sure the asset type aligns with your legacy goals (e.g., pre-tax to charity, Roth/brokerage to children, if appropriate).
4. **Evaluate Roth Conversion Strategy.**
   Revisit whether additional Roth conversions now could reduce future Widow Tax and generational tax exposure. Pay

special attention to the years before Social Security and before the RMD age.

5. **Estimate Your Children's Likely Tax Brackets.**
Consider where your children may be financially when they inherit. Are they likely to be in peak earning years? If so, inherited IRA planning becomes even more important.

6. **Project Estate Growth.**
Run a 20–30 year projection of total net worth under conservative assumptions. Determine whether federal or state estate tax exposure could emerge over time.

7. **Have the Conversation.**
Talk with your spouse—and when appropriate, your children—about expectations. Legacy planning works best when there are no surprises.

If you feel energized by these strategies, that's excellent. If you feel overwhelmed, that's normal too. The math can be meaningful, and the decisions can feel weighty. In the next chapter, we'll discuss how to integrate these moving parts into your overall investment strategy. And in Chapter 10, we'll address Financial Fatigue and the role of a Tax Strategist in helping you execute this plan with clarity and confidence.

More Money, More Problems

Chapter 9
A Better Investing Strategy Creates Better Problems

If you have read *3D Retirement Income*, much of this chapter will feel like a guided refresher. Think of it as a structured summary of the Introduction through Chapter 5 of that book, reframed through the lens of tax planning. If you have not read it yet, I strongly encourage you to do so. You can request a free copy at RetireMentorship.com.

Why dedicate an entire chapter in a tax book to investment philosophy?

Because taxes do not exist in a vacuum.

Your tax return is simply a reflection of your income. Your income is a reflection of your investments. And your long-term after-tax wealth is a reflection of both.

You cannot meaningfully minimize lifetime taxes if you do not first build meaningful wealth. And you cannot build meaningful wealth in retirement without an investment strategy designed for growth, resilience, and flexibility.

There is a warning, however.

Better investment strategies create bigger account balances.

Bigger account balances create larger distributions.

Larger distributions create larger tax bills.

That is not a flaw. That is success.

The goal has never been to pay the least amount of taxes. The goal is to have the most money after taxes over your lifetime and for your heirs. When you combine 3D Retirement Income with intelligent tax planning, you create better problems—higher taxes attached to far higher income, flexibility, generosity, and legacy.

Let's begin with the core problem that derails so many retirements.

The Principal Problem

Most retirees misdiagnose the greatest threat to their financial future.

They believe the primary danger is stock market volatility.

It isn't.

The greatest danger in retirement is insufficient long-term growth.

I call this The Principal Problem.

The Principal Problem occurs when retirees become so focused on preserving their principal that they sacrifice the very growth required to sustain their income for decades.

Think about the psychological shift that happens at retirement. For thirty or forty years, you were accumulating assets. Market declines were inconvenient but tolerable because you were still contributing. Then retirement arrives, paychecks stop, and suddenly your portfolio feels fragile. Instead of being an engine, it feels like a lifeline.

The natural instinct is to protect it.

So many retirees shift heavily into bonds, CDs, annuities, and cash. The account balance stabilizes. The daily swings shrink. It feels safer.

But stability without sufficient growth is not safety. It is slow erosion.

Let's look at the math.

Suppose a couple retires at 65 with $1,000,000 and plans to withdraw $50,000 per year. If inflation averages 3%, that $50,000 must grow to approximately $67,000 by age 75, $90,000 by age 85, and over $120,000 by age 95 just to maintain the same purchasing power.

If their portfolio earns 3–4% in conservative fixed-income investments, and they are withdrawing 5% to start, the margin for error becomes razor-thin. Add taxes to the equation—federal, state, potentially IRMAA—and the portfolio may need to generate 6–7% gross just to maintain spending power after tax.

Inflation compounds quietly. Taxes skim continuously. Longevity stretches the timeline.

The Principal Problem is not losing 20% in a temporary bear market. It is failing to grow enough over 30 years to sustain rising withdrawals.

Short-term volatility feels dangerous because it is visible. Long-term insufficiency feels safe because it is gradual.

But one is temporary.

The other is permanent.

The Principal Problem reframes retirement risk. The question is not, "How do I avoid market fluctuations?" The question is, "How do I build an income that grows faster than inflation, lasts as long as I live, and flexes through downturns?"

That question leads directly to the 3D framework.

3D Retirement Income

In *3D Retirement Income*, I introduced a framework built around three essential dimensions of retirement income: Direction, Duration, and Diversion.

Most retirement plans focus on one dimension—usually Duration. They run Monte Carlo simulations asking, "What are the odds I won't run out of money?" But retirement income is more complex than that.

To thrive in retirement, income must:
- Grow in the right direction.
- Last for the right duration.
- Flex through market disruption.

Let's walk through each dimension.

Direction

Direction asks a simple but powerful question:

Is your retirement income moving upward over time?

Inflation is relentless. Even modest inflation compounds dramatically over multi-decade retirements. At 3%, purchasing power is cut roughly in half in 24 years. At 4%, it halves in 18 years.

If your income is flat, you are effectively receiving a pay cut every year.

Many retirees build portfolios designed to generate "income"—dividends and bond interest—without asking whether that income will grow. A bond paying 4% will continue paying 4%, but it will not increase its payments to keep pace with rising grocery bills, property taxes, or healthcare costs.

Businesses, however, often can.

When you own companies—through diversified equity funds—you participate in their pricing power, productivity growth, and global expansion. Over long periods, corporate earnings have tended to grow faster than inflation. Dividends often rise. Share prices appreciate.

Direction requires meaningful ownership.

This does not mean reckless speculation. It means recognizing that productive assets—businesses—have historically been the most reliable engine for long-term purchasing power growth.

Without Direction, Duration becomes fragile. Without growth, even the most carefully designed withdrawal strategy eventually erodes principal.

Direction is what keeps your retirement income climbing rather than shrinking.

Duration

Duration asks:

Will your income last as long as you and your spouse do?

Longevity risk is frequently underestimated. A healthy 65-year-old couple has a significant probability that at least one spouse lives into their nineties. That is potentially 25–35 years of required income.

Duration is strengthened through diversification across time, asset classes, and income sources.

Social Security provides inflation-adjusted lifetime income and acts as a longevity hedge. Delaying benefits can significantly increase survivor income for the remaining spouse.

A disciplined withdrawal strategy helps prevent overspending in early years.

Growth assets support the portfolio's ability to replenish withdrawals.

Here is the paradox: overly conservative portfolios may weaken Duration. If returns are too low, withdrawals consume principal faster than anticipated. The portfolio may survive market downturns but fail quietly due to insufficient compounding.

Duration is not about eliminating risk. It is about sustaining resilience over decades.

Diversion

Diversion answers the third essential question:

Can your income flex during market downturns without permanently impairing growth?

Markets do not move in straight lines. Historically, declines of 20% or more occur regularly. Bear markets are normal features of long-term investing.

If you are forced to sell large portions of equities during downturns to fund living expenses, you lock in losses and reduce the portfolio's ability to recover.

Diversion requires liquidity and strategic segmentation.

It may involve maintaining a reserve of lower-volatility assets—cash, short-term bonds, or other stabilizing holdings—that can fund spending temporarily when equities decline.

It may involve dynamic withdrawal adjustments—slightly reducing discretionary spending during downturns.

It may involve tax planning strategies—such as harvesting losses in brokerage accounts or converting less during volatile years.

Diversion is not about avoiding downturns. It is about navigating them intelligently so Direction and Duration remain intact.

When Direction, Duration, and Diversion work together, retirement income becomes multidimensional and resilient. Remove one, and the structure weakens.

Owning Your Retirement

A foundational principle in *3D Retirement Income* is the distinction between being an owner and being a loaner.

TAX SAVING STRATEGIES - 179

Loaners lend money to governments and corporations. They receive interest in return. Bonds, CDs, Treasuries, savings accounts, and money market funds fall into this category.

Owners purchase equity in businesses. They participate in growth and profits. Stocks, mutual funds, and ETFs represent ownership.

Both have roles in a diversified portfolio. But they behave very differently over time.

Loaners trade upside for predictability. Owners trade predictability for upside.

Historically, ownership has outperformed lending over long periods because businesses innovate, expand, and adjust prices with inflation. Lending produces fixed returns that may lag inflation.

In retirement, this distinction becomes critical.

If your portfolio becomes dominated by lending, you may feel stable—but you risk stagnation. If inflation averages 3–4% and your bonds yield 3–4%, you are treading water before taxes.

Ownership, however, introduces volatility. Stock prices fluctuate daily. Headlines amplify fear. But volatility is the price of growth.

Over 30-year periods, broad equity markets have historically produced returns significantly above inflation. That growth supports Direction and strengthens Duration.

From a tax perspective, ownership often enjoys structural advantages.

Long-term capital gains and qualified dividends are taxed at preferential rates—0%, 15%, or 20% federally, depending on taxable income, plus potential NIIT. Interest income is taxed at ordinary income rates.

Ownership also allows for tax management techniques such as tax-loss harvesting and tax-gain harvesting, which we discussed in Chapter 5 of this book.

Owning your retirement means embracing productive assets as the primary engine of long-term income growth, while strategically using lending assets to provide stability and Diversion.

It also requires emotional discipline.

Short-term volatility is not evidence of failure. It is a normal feature of ownership. Retirees who panic during downturns often undermine the very strategy designed to protect them.

Ownership, when aligned with 3D principles and integrated tax planning, becomes a powerful wealth engine.

Red Bucket, Blue Bucket

To make these concepts tangible, *3D Retirement Income* introduces the Red Bucket and Blue Bucket framework.

The Red Bucket represents assets exposed to stock market volatility—primarily equities and equity-based funds.

The Blue Bucket represents more stable assets—cash, short-term bonds, and other lower-volatility holdings.

Many retirees instinctively want to shrink the Red Bucket dramatically at retirement. They equate retirement with safety and safety with stability.

But eliminating or severely shrinking the Red Bucket sacrifices Direction.

The goal is not to eliminate volatility. The goal is to manage it strategically.

The Blue Bucket exists to fund near-term spending needs—often one to five years of expenses—without requiring equity sales during downturns.

If markets decline, withdrawals can come from the Blue Bucket while the Red Bucket recovers.

When markets rise, gains from the Red Bucket can replenish the Blue Bucket.

This disciplined interplay supports Diversion while preserving long-term growth.

Over decades, the Red Bucket drives wealth expansion. The Blue Bucket protects against sequence-of-returns risk in the short term.

Too much Blue Bucket and the portfolio may stagnate.

Too much Red Bucket and emotional reactions during downturns may cause poor decisions.

The balance is intentional and dynamic.

Now connect this to taxes.

As the Red Bucket grows, it produces capital gains and dividends. Eventually, distributions—RMDs, withdrawals, rebalancing—create taxable events.

That is not a failure.

It is evidence of growth.

A larger Red Bucket will often produce larger tax bills. But those tax bills are attached to larger account values, higher income potential, and greater flexibility.

That is a better problem than low taxes attached to insufficient income.

Quantifying the Difference: Loaner vs. Owner Over 30 Years

It may be helpful to put real numbers behind what we've been discussing. Let's compare two hypothetical couples, each retiring at age 65 with $1,000,000 and withdrawing $50,000 in year one, increasing that withdrawal by 3% annually to keep up with inflation.

Doug & Joan adopt a highly conservative strategy. Their portfolio earns an average of 4% per year before taxes. Chuck & Diane adopt a 3D-oriented strategy with meaningful ownership exposure, earning an average annual return of 8% before taxes. We will simplify by assuming taxes reduce net returns modestly and that both couples are in similar tax brackets over time. The goal is directional clarity, not precision modeling.

Doug & Joan – 4% Average Return

Starting portfolio: $1,000,000. Initial withdrawal: $50,000. Withdrawal growth: 3% annually. Average return: 4%.

In the early years, the math appears workable. The portfolio earns roughly $40,000 in year one and distributes $50,000, with the shortfall covered by dipping into principal. Because withdrawals grow with inflation while returns remain modest, the gap widens over time. By their late seventies, the portfolio is shrinking meaningfully, and by their mid-eighties, the risk of depletion becomes very real depending on the sequence of returns.

Taxes remain relatively modest in absolute dollars—but so does long-term wealth. The primary concern for Doug & Joan is sustainability rather than optimization.

Chuck & Diane – 8% Average Return

Starting portfolio: $1,000,000. Initial withdrawal: $50,000. Withdrawal growth: 3% annually. Average return: 8%.

In year one, the portfolio earns roughly $80,000. After withdrawing $50,000, the account still grows. Over time, even as withdrawals increase with inflation, compounding works in their favor. By age 75, their portfolio may be significantly larger than at retirement, and by age 85, even after decades of withdrawals, it may still exceed the original balance.

At age 95, there is a strong probability that meaningful assets remain. Chuck & Diane will likely realize larger capital gains, experience larger RMDs, potentially trigger IRMAA, and pay more absolute dollars in tax over their lifetime. But they will also have greater income flexibility, larger charitable gifting capacity, stronger survivor protection, and more legacy potential.

The difference in lifetime wealth between a 4% and 8% return over 30 years is staggering. At 4%, $1,000,000 grows to roughly $3.2 million over 30 years before withdrawals. At 8%, $1,000,000 grows to over $10 million over 30 years before withdrawals. Even after substantial withdrawals and taxes, the ownership-oriented strategy has dramatically more room for error.

This is what I mean by better problems. Doug & Joan worry about running out, while Chuck & Diane worry about managing tax brackets efficiently. I know which problem I would rather solve.

Red Bucket, Blue Bucket in Action: A Downturn Scenario

Let's now walk through a real-world sequence-of-returns example using the Red and Blue Bucket framework.

Assume a couple retires with:
- $800,000 in the Red Bucket (equities)
- $200,000 in the Blue Bucket (cash and short-term bonds)

They need $60,000 per year in withdrawals.

Year One – Market Decline of 25%

The Red Bucket falls from $800,000 to $600,000.

The Blue Bucket remains stable at $200,000.

Instead of panicking and selling equities at depressed values, they withdraw their $60,000 entirely from the Blue Bucket.

After withdrawal:
- Red Bucket: $600,000
- Blue Bucket: $140,000

No equities were sold at a loss.

Year Two – Market Remains Flat

They again withdraw $60,000 from the Blue Bucket.
- Red Bucket: $600,000
- Blue Bucket: $80,000

Still no forced equity sales.

Year Three – Market Recovers 20%

The Red Bucket grows from $600,000 to $720,000.

Now they rebalance.

They trim $100,000 from the Red Bucket to replenish the Blue Bucket.

- Red Bucket: $620,000
- Blue Bucket: $180,000

Over a three-year volatile period, they avoided selling equities during the downturn and allowed recovery to occur before rebalancing.

This is Diversion in practice.

Now layer in tax planning.

During Year One, when the market declined 25%, they may have harvested tax losses in their brokerage Red Bucket holdings. Those losses can offset future gains or reduce ordinary income by up to $3,000 annually.

During recovery years, they may strategically realize gains up to the top of the 0% or 15% capital gains bracket.

During especially low-income years, they may perform modest Roth conversions without triggering IRMAA.

The Red and Blue Buckets are not just behavioral tools—they are tax tools.

Downturns create loss-harvesting opportunities.

Recovery years create rebalancing and gain-harvesting opportunities.

Strong growth years create opportunities for charitable gifting through appreciated stock.

This dynamic interplay between investment structure and tax strategy is where the real power lies.

Investment Growth Fuels Tax Strategy

Let's connect this directly to the earlier chapters in this book.

A larger Red Bucket creates larger potential Roth conversion windows in early retirement years before RMDs begin.

A growing brokerage account creates opportunities for tax-loss harvesting during downturns and tax-gain harvesting in low-income years.

Appreciated assets become powerful charitable tools when bundled with deduction strategies or donor-advised funds.

Larger traditional account balances may create RMD challenges—but they also create QCD opportunities.

Without growth, many of these strategies barely matter.

If your portfolio is stagnant, there are no significant gains to harvest, no meaningful conversions to manage, and no appreciated shares to donate.

But when growth is present, tax planning becomes proactive rather than reactive.

You shift from worrying about depletion to optimizing brackets.

You move from scarcity management to strategic abundance.

That is the shift this chapter is designed to make.

More growth does not eliminate taxes.

It creates choices.

And with wise planning, those choices allow you to minimize lifetime taxation while maximizing lifetime and legacy wealth.

More Money, Better Problems

The entire premise of this chapter can be summarized simply.

If you underinvest and earn 3–4% long term, you may avoid volatility—but you will likely struggle with longevity and inflation risk.

If you invest with ownership discipline and earn 7–9% over long horizons, you will experience volatility—but you dramatically increase the probability of surplus rather than shortage.

Yes, surplus creates tax complexity.

Yes, surplus can trigger IRMAA.

Yes, surplus can push you into higher brackets.

But surplus also allows you to:

- Control the timing of income.
- Fund charitable goals generously.
- Protect a surviving spouse.
- Leave tax-efficient inheritances.
- Sleep at night knowing depletion risk is low.

You cannot tax-plan your way out of insufficient growth.

But you can growth-plan your way into better tax problems.

That is the integration of 3D Retirement Income and this book's tax strategies.

More Money. Better Problems. And a plan designed to handle both.

If you underinvest and earn 3–4% long term, you may avoid volatility—but you will likely struggle with longevity and inflation risk. If you invest with ownership discipline and earn 7–9% over long horizons, you will experience volatility—but you dramatically increase the probability of surplus rather than shortage.

Surplus does create tax complexity. It can trigger IRMAA, push you into higher brackets, and require careful income coordination. But surplus also allows you to control the timing of income, fund charitable goals generously, protect a surviving spouse, leave tax-efficient inheritances, and sleep at night knowing depletion risk is low.

You cannot tax-plan your way out of insufficient growth, but you can growth-plan your way into better tax problems. That is the integration of 3D Retirement Income and this book's tax strategies—intentional ownership combined with intentional tax management over a lifetime.

Chapter Summary
- Retirement risk is often misunderstood. The greatest long-term danger is not market volatility but insufficient growth to sustain rising income needs over decades. The Principal Problem occurs when retirees overemphasize stability and underemphasize compounding, sacrificing the growth required to outpace inflation and taxes.
- The 3D Retirement Income framework addresses this challenge through three dimensions. Direction ensures income grows faster than inflation. Duration ensures income lasts as long as you and your spouse do. Diversion ensures your income can flex during market downturns without permanently impairing long-term growth.
- Owning productive businesses through equities has historically provided the strongest engine for long-term Direction, while lending assets provide stability and Diversion. The Red Bucket and Blue Bucket framework helps retirees balance growth and stability while supporting both behavioral discipline and tax efficiency.
- Stronger investment returns often create larger tax bills. However, they also create greater flexibility, generosity, survivor protection, and legacy potential. The goal is not to avoid taxes by suppressing growth. The goal is to build sub-

stantial wealth and then manage taxes intentionally over a lifetime.
- More money does create more complexity. But those are better problems than running out of money.

Action Items

1. Reassess Your True Risk.

   Ask yourself whether your current investment strategy prioritizes short-term stability over long-term growth. Are you protecting principal at the expense of purchasing power 15–25 years from now?

2. Evaluate Direction, Duration, and Diversion.

   For each dimension, write down how your current portfolio addresses it. Does your income grow? Is it likely to last through age 90–95? Do you have a clear plan for market downturns?

3. Review Your Red and Blue Buckets.

   Identify which assets represent growth (Red Bucket) and which provide short-term stability (Blue Bucket). Do you have a disciplined plan for replenishing one from the other during market cycles?

4. Integrate Investment and Tax Planning.

   Look at your projected RMDs, Roth conversion strategy, brokerage account growth, and charitable goals together—not separately. Growth creates tax events; planning turns them into opportunities.

5. Get the Full Framework.

   If you have not already done so, request your free copy of *3D*

Retirement Income at RetireMentorship.com. This chapter is a summary. The full book walks step-by-step through the principles, math, and behavioral frameworks behind building income that outpaces inflation, outlives you, and outperforms conventional strategies.

6. **Decide Whether You Will DIY or Delegate.**
If this chapter energized you, begin building your integrated plan. If it overwhelmed you, that is normal. In the next chapter, we will discuss how to implement these strategies effectively—either on your own or with a professional who understands both investing and taxes.

A Tax Strategist

Chapter 10
Working with a Fiduciary Tax Planner & Preparer

If you've made it this far, you've done more tax planning than most Americans will ever attempt, and that alone sets you apart. Most couples never move beyond tax preparation, yet you have worked through buckets, brackets, stacking rules, IRMAA thresholds, Social Security taxation, charitable sequencing, Roth conversions, brokerage optimization, and investment structure. You now understand that your 1040 is not an isolated document but a summary of your entire financial life.

In Chapter 1, we clarified the goal: not to pay the least in taxes this year, but to have the most money after taxes over your lifetime. From there, we examined how Traditional accounts, Roth accounts, brokerage accounts, Medicare premiums, Required Minimum Distributions, and equity growth all interact. Each lever you pull moves three others, which is why tax planning for couples over fifty is not a tactic but a coordinated system.

Knowing these strategies and implementing them with precision are two different skill sets. Understanding Roth conversion theory is one thing; modeling it across 25 years of retirement, survivor brackets, and IRMAA tiers is another. This chapter exists to help you decide whether you will master that integration yourself or partner with someone who already has.

Financial Fatigue

The strategies in this book could make you $500,000, and in some cases, far more. More specifically, implementing these strategies could reasonably save more than $100,000 in unnecessary taxes for every $1,000,000 of retirement assets you have. When those tax savings are reinvested and compounded alongside the equity ownership strategies from Chapter 9, the lifetime difference can easily climb into the six- or seven-figure range.

That statement is not marketing hype; it is math. A persistent 2–3% reduction in lifetime effective tax drag, applied to millions of dollars of distributions and growth, compounds the same way investment returns do. Avoid poorly timed Roth conversions, unnecessary IRMAA surcharges, excessive Social Security taxation, inefficient charitable sequencing, and asset location mistakes, and the cumulative effect becomes dramatic over 20 to 30 years.

However, the honest truth is that these strategies are not simple. At some point while reading this book, you likely felt the weight of stacking formulas, provisional income calculations, two-year IRMAA lookbacks, RMD projections, and survivor bracket compression. The deeper you went, the more interconnected everything became, and what started as "saving taxes" began to resemble a graduate-level systems problem.

That experience is what I call **Financial Fatigue**. Financial Fatigue occurs when the cost of thinking feels heavier than the cost of inaction, even though inaction is far more expensive over time. The danger is not that you misunderstand one rule; the danger is that you decide the complexity is not worth engaging and quietly default to whatever happens.

You absolutely can implement these strategies yourself. If you are willing to learn the rules, purchase professional-grade modeling software, build long-term projections, update them annually, and coordinate every decision across taxes, investments, Medicare, and estate planning, you can capture the value. But let's quantify what that realistically requires.

To gain foundational competence comparable to that of a trained professional, you would need education equivalent to that of a comprehensive financial planner with tax specialization. CFP® coursework typically requires around 300 hours of study, and a tax credential such as the Enrolled Agent designation often demands another 150–200 hours of focused preparation. Even if you are efficient and highly capable, you are likely investing 400 or more hours to build a base level of structured knowledge.

Next, consider software. Professional financial planning platforms that properly model Roth conversions, IRMAA thresholds, Social Security taxation, and multi-decade projections often cost thousands of dollars per year. Conservatively estimate $5,000 for access and training, plus another 50 hours to learn how to use the tools accurately and build your own model.

Now assign value to your time. If your earning power has been $100,000 per year, that equates to roughly $50 per hour across a 2,000-hour work year. 450 hours at $50 per hour equals $22,500 in opportunity cost. Add approximately $15,000 for education and software, and your total DIY investment approaches $37,500 before you even factor in experience.

If you enjoy this work and want a second career in retirement tax strategy, that investment may be rational. Spending $25,000–$50,000 of time and money to potentially capture $500,000–$1,000,000 of lifetime value can make mathematical sense. But most couples do not want a second career in tax law;

they want clarity, confidence, and more time with the people and pursuits that matter most.

If you can hire a competent strategist for $5,000–$25,000 to design and guide a plan that saves you $100,000 or more, that is not an expense but a trade. The relevant question is not "Can I do this?" but "Where is my time best spent?" Every hour devoted to mastering Medicare premium tiers is an hour not invested in your spouse, grandchildren, church, travel, or meaningful work.

Delegation is not weakness; it is leverage. The only requirement is that if you delegate, you must do so wisely and intentionally rather than casually.

The Professional Limitations

What makes retirement tax planning uniquely complex is that it requires dual expertise. It lives at the intersection of advanced tax knowledge and comprehensive financial planning, yet most professionals are trained in only one of those disciplines. When advice remains siloed, integration suffers, and integration is exactly what this stage of life demands.

Tax planning for couples over fifty must account for investment allocation, withdrawal sequencing, Social Security timing, Medicare premiums, estate coordination, and long-term projections. A professional who understands only the tax code without understanding the broader plan will inevitably answer questions in isolation. Likewise, a planner who understands investments but lacks tax depth may avoid specific guidance precisely where it matters most.

Tax Expertise

Let's begin with tax expertise and clarify the differences between various credentials. The public often assumes that anyone who prepares tax returns has equivalent training, but the regulatory spectrum is far wider than most realize.

Tax Preparers

To prepare federal tax returns for compensation, an individual must obtain a Preparer Tax Identification Number (PTIN) from the IRS. The requirements for a PTIN are minimal, and there is no universal education mandate or comprehensive licensing exam required to begin preparing returns. Many seasonal preparers at large chains operate under this framework.

This does not mean they are incompetent, but it does mean their role is typically compliance-focused. They gather W-2s and 1099s, input historical data, and ensure last year's return is filed correctly. The emphasis is on accurately reporting what has already occurred, not on proactive lifetime modeling.

If your only annual tax interaction is dropping documents off in March and signing where indicated, you are participating in tax preparation, not tax planning. Preparation is backward-looking by definition, while planning must be forward-looking and integrated.

Enrolled Agents (EA)

An Enrolled Agent is federally licensed by the IRS and must pass a rigorous three-part Special Enrollment Examination covering individual taxation, business taxation, and representation. Alternatively, an individual may qualify through prior experience as an IRS employee in certain roles. The exam is tax-specific and focuses deeply on the Internal Revenue Code rather than auditing or financial accounting.

EAs are required to complete continuing education, including ethics, and they possess unlimited rights to represent taxpayers before the IRS. In the realm of personal income tax law, a strong EA is highly trained and often specializes specifically in the nuances that affect retirees.

Certified Public Accountant (CPA)

Certified Public Accountants are licensed at the state level and must complete substantial education requirements, typically including 150 college credit hours, and pass the Uniform CPA Examination. The CPA credential covers auditing, financial accounting, business law, and taxation. Because the exam is broad, many CPAs focus their careers on corporate audits, financial statements, or business consulting rather than personal retirement tax strategy.

A CPA who specializes in individual taxation can be outstanding. However, the credential alone does not guarantee deep experience in retirement-specific issues such as Roth conversion sequencing, IRMAA planning, or survivor bracket compression.

Tax Preparer Limitations

Even highly competent EAs and CPAs face structural limitations when operating without integrated financial planning knowledge. Tax professionals are trained primarily in statutory interpretation, compliance, and representation, not in portfolio construction, income sequencing, or long-term retirement modeling.

If a tax professional does not deeply understand how a Roth conversion affects Social Security taxation, Medicare premiums two years later, equity allocation, and legacy distribution, then their advice is technically accurate but strategically incomplete. Tax law cannot be applied optimally without understanding the broader financial architecture it influences.

Financial Planning

Now let's examine the financial planning side of the equation. The financial services industry contains a wide range of licenses and designations, many of which sound impressive but vary dramatically in rigor and scope.

Insurance Licensed Professionals

Some professionals operate primarily under state insurance licenses. To obtain a life insurance license, candidates typically pass a state exam, with first-time pass rates often ranging from 60–70%. The study period can be measured in weeks rather than years, and the curriculum focuses on product knowledge and regulatory compliance rather than integrated retirement planning.

Insurance products are frequently marketed as tax solutions, including indexed universal life or certain annuities positioned as "tax-free retirement" vehicles. As discussed in Chapter 3, many of these strategies prioritize product commissions over long-term tax efficiency and investment performance. When the barrier to entry is modest and compensation is commission-based, caution is warranted.

Investment Licensed Professionals

Investment professionals may hold licenses such as the Series 6, 7, 65, or 66. Pass rates for these exams commonly fall between

60–75%, and the content focuses heavily on securities regulation, product structure, and compliance rules. These exams do not constitute comprehensive education in retirement tax planning or multi-decade modeling.

There is also a critical distinction between professionals licensed to sell investment products and those registered to provide ongoing fiduciary advice. Selling a mutual fund or annuity under a suitability standard is not the same as delivering integrated retirement planning under a fiduciary obligation.

Financial Designations

There are more than 200 financial designations in existence, ranging from rigorous to purely marketing-driven. The Chartered Life Underwriter (CLU), for example, offers in-depth insurance education but does not equate to broad retirement tax integration. Evaluating a designation requires understanding what the curriculum actually covers rather than assuming the acronym guarantees comprehensive expertise.

Certified Financial Planner (CFP®)

The CFP® designation is widely regarded as the gold standard for comprehensive financial planning. Candidates must complete extensive coursework covering investments, retirement planning, insurance, estate planning, and tax concepts. They must pass a demanding multi-hour exam, accumulate professional experience, complete continuing education, and adhere to fiduciary standards when providing advice.

The CFP® curriculum emphasizes integration. It teaches how decisions in one area affect all others, which is essential when coordinating Roth conversions, Social Security, IRMAA thresholds, and investment growth. The Chartered Financial Consultant (ChFC) is a close alternative and similarly robust in scope.

Financial Planner Limitations

Even CFP® professionals may face limitations. Some work within firms that prohibit giving specific tax advice, restricting them to general education rather than actionable guidance. Others may understand tax concepts broadly but lack the credentials or experience to implement complex strategies or prepare returns.

A planner without tax specialization may design thoughtful projections but defer critical tax decisions to a CPA who lacks investment integration. That handoff can create fragmentation precisely where coordination is required.

The Tax Planning Conundrum

The result of these professional silos is a familiar loop. You ask your investment advisor whether you should convert $50,000 to a Roth this year, and they respond that it depends on your tax situation and recommend that you consult your CPA. You ask your CPA the same question, and they respond that they lack visibility into your long-term retirement projections and recommend that you consult your advisor.

Meanwhile, December 31 arrives, and the opportunity closes. If you rely solely on tax software, you are effectively your own CPA and financial planner without access to professional modeling tools. This fragmentation is one of the primary reasons couples over fifty overpay taxes despite having competent professionals involved.

Retirement tax planning requires integration, and integration requires someone accountable for both sides of the equation.

The Tax Planning Solution: A Fiduciary Tax Strategist

If your objective is to maximize after-tax wealth without investing hundreds of hours mastering the code, you need a Fiduciary Tax Strategist. That phrase is not marketing language; it represents a specific combination of credentials, training, and compensation alignment.

A Certified Financial Planner

A competent strategist must possess comprehensive knowledge of financial planning. Tax decisions cannot be evaluated apart from retirement income sequencing, portfolio allocation, Social Security optimization, Medicare planning, and estate coordination. A CFP® or ChFC designation signals that the professional has been trained to evaluate those interdependencies systematically.

A Tax Specialty

In addition to comprehensive planning credentials, your strategist should hold a tax-focused designation such as EA, CPA, or an advanced tax certification. This ensures they can interpret the Internal Revenue Code accurately and implement strategies rather than merely discuss them conceptually.

Designations such as Certified Tax Specialist (CTS) or Tax Planning Certified Professional (TPCP) indicate a further commitment to proactive tax-reduction strategies. While these credentials vary in recognition, they often emphasize forward-looking planning rather than simple compliance.

The essential principle is that your strategist must understand both the tax code and the retirement plan deeply enough to integrate them without deferring critical decisions elsewhere.

A Fee-Only Fiduciary

Compensation drives behavior, which is why the fee structure is not a minor detail but a foundational requirement. A fiduciary is legally obligated to act in your best interest when providing advice, whereas a suitability standard merely requires that a product be appropriate, not optimal.

Many professionals operate under a dual standard, acting as fiduciaries when managing investments and switching to suitability when recommending commission-based insurance products.

Clients often remain unaware of when that shift occurs because it is buried within lengthy agreements.

Fee-based advisors may charge planning fees while also earning commissions. Fee-only advisors, by contrast, are compensated solely by client-paid fees and do not sell commission products. That structural alignment eliminates a category of conflict entirely and clarifies whose interests are being served.

When I began my career, our planning contract stated that we were fiduciaries during the planning process. Deeper in the document, however, it disclosed that, when recommending insurance products, we were acting as representatives of the insurance company rather than as fiduciaries. Clients believed they had a fiduciary relationship throughout, but the legal reality was more nuanced.

Fee-only eliminates that ambiguity. It ensures that advice is not influenced by product incentives, and it creates clarity around accountability.

How to Find a Fiduciary Tax Strategist

If you determine that delegation is the wisest course, there are several practical pathways.

Work with Me

You are reading this book because I have devoted my career to integrating retirement planning and tax strategy. I am a Fee-Only Fiduciary CFP® and Enrolled Agent, and my firm specializes in helping couples over fifty design coordinated, forward-looking plans.

Our process follows what I call the 3D Evaluation Process. First, we meet to discover whether there is mutual fit and whether we can meaningfully improve your situation. Second, we provide a no-cost demonstration of specific strategies we would use to enhance your outcomes. Third, we clearly outline the scope of work and fees, and give you time to decide without pressure.

The objective is clarity, not salesmanship.

Other Tax Strategists

If geography or preference leads you elsewhere, you can explore the Fiduciary Financial Planning Network at FiduciaryFinancialPlanning.net. Members of this network are Fee-Only fiduciaries, typically hold the CFP® designation, and often possess tax specialization or access to dedicated tax experts. They also share a philosophy aligned with disciplined equity ownership and integrated planning.

Other Fee-Only Fiduciaries

A broader directory of Fee-Only fiduciary planners can be found at FeeOnlyNetwork.com. While not every professional in that directory will possess tax credentials, the fee-only requirement helps eliminate commission conflicts. If tax expertise is not present internally, confirm that the planner coordinates closely with a tax specialist rather than operating in isolation.

Conclusion

Tax planning at this stage of life is not about tricks or loopholes; it is about disciplined integration across decades. You have seen how Roth conversions interact with Social Security taxation, how brokerage gains can trigger IRMAA, how charitable giving can reduce RMD exposure, and how equity growth creates both larger tax bills and larger opportunities.

The question before you is not whether these strategies work but whether they will be implemented with precision and consistency. If you enjoy modeling scenarios and maintaining projections annually, you can climb the learning curve and manage the process yourself. If Financial Fatigue is already whispering that you would rather focus elsewhere, leverage a professional who meets the standards outlined in this chapter.

Either path requires intention. Your largest lifetime expense deserves planning that is equally thoughtful and coordinated.

Chapter Summary
- The objective of tax planning is to maximize lifetime after-tax wealth, not to minimize a single year's tax bill.
- Financial Fatigue is normal when confronting complex, integrated decisions.
- Effective retirement tax planning requires both comprehensive financial planning expertise and advanced tax knowledge.
- Many professionals operate in silos, which can create fragmentation and missed opportunities.
- A Fiduciary Tax Strategist should hold a CFP® (or comparable) designation, possess tax credentials, and operate as a Fee-Only fiduciary.
- Compensation structure matters because incentives influence behavior.

Action Items
1. Decide intentionally whether you will pursue full DIY mastery or delegate to a qualified professional.
2. If working with an advisor, verify that they hold a comprehensive planning designation and a tax credential.
3. Confirm that their compensation structure is truly Fee-Only and fiduciary at all times.
4. Ensure that at least one multi-year tax projection is built and updated annually to coordinate Roth conversions, Social Security timing, and IRMAA thresholds.
5. If you desire guidance from my firm, begin the 3D Evaluation Process at RetireMentorship.com and determine whether a partnership is appropriate.

Intentional planning will not eliminate taxes, but it will ensure you never pay more than necessary.

www.ingramcontent.com/pod-product-compliance
Lightning Source LLC
LaVergne TN
LVHW020426070526
838199LV00004B/300